KEEPING OUR KIDS SAFE
AND OUT OF TROUBLE

KEEPING OUR KIDS SAFE
AND OUT OF TROUBLE

What a criminal defense attorney tells
his kids and wants you to tell yours

SCOTT LIMMER

TABLE OF CONTENTS

Acknowledgements 7

Preface: A Few Notes Before We Start 9

Introduction   11

Chapter 1:   Fake IDs 17

Chapter 2:   Drinking at Home 23

Chapter 3:   Driving While Intoxicated...................... 30

Chapter 4:   Cannabis... 37

Chapter 5:   Distracted Driving 43

Chapter 6:   How Drivers Should Deal with the Police 48

Chapter 7:   Talking to the Police 54

Chapter 8:   What Happens When Someone Gets Arrested 62

Chapter 9:   Juvenile Court 74

Chapter 10:   Student Rights in Schools 80

Chapter 11:   Social Media and Cell Phones 89

Chapter 12:   High School Disciplinary Process 98

Chapter 13:   Greek Life and Hazing 107

Chapter 14:   Drugs and Alcohol in College.................... 114

Chapter 15:   Plagiarism....................................... 121

Chapter 16:   Academic Misconduct 129

Chapter 17:   Title IX and Sex Offenses 133

Chapter 18:   The College Disciplinary Process 143

Chapter 19:   Helping Students with Disabilities 154

Chapter 20:   What Breaking the Rules Means
for Your Kid's Future 160

Conclusion: Be Smart 167

References   169

ACKNOWLEDGMENTS

I am grateful to the following people for helping me to make this book a reality.

First and foremost, to my wife, Gail. We have been side by side for 27 years, raising two daughters and have dealt with many of the issues addressed in this book. Without your support and faith in me, I would never have been able to start my own law practice, write this book, or be a parent. Love you, Gail.

To my daughters, Julia, and Danielle, who inspired me to write this book. In the first years of representing younger clients, I had wondered what I would tell you both when you were old enough to engage in risky behavior. Eventually, I spoke honestly, and you both listened. I have no doubt you both will make mistakes and find yourselves in uncomfortable situations, but I believe you both have the tools to make good decisions. Love you.

To my parents, for giving me the freedom to make mistakes and allowing me to learn from them.

To all my high school and college friends, who participated with me in some of the activities I write about: we had fun, didn't get into trouble (mostly), and were extremely fortunate there was no social media to memorialize every mistake we made.

To Oscar Michelen, my podcast co-host and friend, for setting an amazing example of what an attorney should strive to be.

To Mark Potashnick, for always taking the time to help a young lawyer whenever he needed the advice of a seasoned practitioner. I am fortunate to have you as a mentor.

To Lee Rosen, this book doesn't happen without you. Period. The guidance you have given me over my career to push the boundaries of what a lawyer can be has been invaluable. Learning from you and the other lawyers at the Rosen Institute helps guide my professional life.

To The First Resource BNI group, walking into a diner 10 years ago, wondering what I was doing in a room full of "networkers," is one of the better decisions I have ever made. Not only did this group help me become a better "networker" but I have been lucky enough to form lasting friendships that mean the world to me.

To all the criminal defense practitioners and to any lawyer who tries to help people in trouble, who does whatever they can to try to help their clients—it's not easy to know that your client's future or freedom depends on you. I am in awe of your dedication and commitment.

I have been practicing in the Nassau County Criminal Courts for almost 30 years. To all the lawyers, judges, court officers and clerks, court reporters, interpreters, and other court personnel, it has been an honor to have shared courtrooms with all of you, and I look forward to sharing many more.

And to all my past, current, and future clients, I am fortunate to be able to help those in situations that may affect the rest of your lives. I am honored and humbled by the people who have allowed me to advocate for fairness or reasonableness on their behalf.

PREFACE:
A FEW NOTES BEFORE WE START

HOW TO USE THIS BOOK

This book is not meant to be read in one sitting and put in the bookcase (or deleted from Kindle), to be forgotten about. This book is for you to refer to as needed, especially if you have kids who are approaching an age when they might have to deal with some of the issues I write about. As parents, you can choose to read a few relevant chapters with your teen and help them learn how to make good choices so as to avoid potentially serious consequences of certain actions. And while I hope that you never have to seek legal counsel or guidance about how to manage a disciplinary or criminal incident, if you do, the information and guidance offered here is intended to help you move forward through the process.

THE SCOPE OF MY PRACTICE

The information in this book is based on my experiences in the specific jurisdictions where I practice. When I discuss criminal or juvenile cases, the relevant law is New York State law. My high school discipline practice is restricted to a number of school districts on Long Island, New York. They all have similar rules but different thoughts about punishment and seriousness. I also advise students in college disciplinary cases around the United States, and each school has its own Code of Conduct. Many of the laws I have dealt with in my jurisdictions will most likely be similar to those you encounter.

MY VIEWPOINT

This is a book about how to help kids stay out of trouble and also about what to do when they *are* in trouble, from my perspective. My perspective is about trying to help the person who is in trouble, and I will relay as much of that information as I can. Regardless of my clients' actions, they all deserve the same vigorous defense. I do not discount the experience and trauma of victims or complainants; however, that is not where my experience lies, and so I cannot give expert advice on that topic, but rather on my client's defense.

USE OF GENDER-BASED PRONOUNS

The use of gender pronouns in this book varies with respect to the situations I describe. No assumptions should be made due to the use of a specific pronoun.

LEGAL ADVICE

Please remember: I am not giving you specific legal advice regarding your specific situation. The information provided in this book does not, and is not intended to, constitute legal advice; it is for general informational purposes only.

CONTENT WARNING

I would like to make all readers aware that Chapter 17, Title IX and Sex Offenses contain descriptions of alleged non-consensual intimate situations. It is possible that something you read during that chapter will trigger an emotional response, whether or not you have experienced non-consensual intimate situations yourself.

INTRODUCTION

It's 1987. I'm an 18-year-old freshman in college hanging out in my dorm room after class one afternoon. To my great surprise, a flaming roll of toilet paper comes flying into my room from our suite's common area. I jump up and stomp the thing out, but not in time. The fire alarm has already gone off.

I don't know who lit the toilet paper on fire, or who threw the thing, or what the consequences will be, but I do know that I've done nothing wrong. Still, I've got a sense of foreboding that makes that trip down 21 flights of stairs with the fire alarm blaring a long, long walk.

When I get to the ground level, the Resident Assistant (our RA) pulls me and my five suitemates aside and tells us to sit down and wait. Soon enough, the police show up. A cop points to me and tells me to come with him. At this point, I'm thinking, "Okay, I'll tell my story, get it all cleared up, and then get back to normal." So, I pop up out of my seat and stride over to the police car. The officer looks at me with a bemused grin and says, "No, son. Come here." Then he handcuffs me and puts me in the car.

At this point, I realize that maybe, just maybe, I'm in some trouble. I know I did nothing wrong, but I am in the back of a police car in handcuffs, so things are not looking good.

At the precinct, the cops leave me in a room for an hour. Finally, another cop comes in and starts questioning me. I tell him the whole story, every single detail I can think of, and explain that I really don't know who did it. I'm as cooperative as I can be.

But the cop isn't having it. He tells me that the other guys are trying to blame it on me, so I'd better tell him who did it. He leaves and then comes back a little while later with a piece of paper and tells me to sign it. It's a statement that says I saw the person who lit the

11

toilet paper on fire. I tell the officer I can't sign it, because I didn't see who lit it, because I was in my bedroom and the perpetrator was in the suite common room at the time. I couldn't understand why the police were trying to solicit a false statement from me.

After a few hours, the cops let me go. At this point, I'm relieved I wasn't arrested, but I'm exhausted. All I want to do is go back to my dorm room and take a nap. But when I finally make it to my room, I don't find sleep, I find a note on my door from the RA. I go to see her, and she hands me a letter that says the school is bringing me up on charges, and that I have a hearing in three days. Until the hearing, I have to stay off-campus.

I am beyond frustrated! The cops let me go, so I thought I was in the clear. But the RA stands firm. I have to go. I'm escorted off-campus. I drop my stuff at a friend's place, march right back on campus to the Student Conduct Office and plead with them to explain what is happening. Instead, they hand me a pamphlet and tell me I've got 15 minutes to get off-campus, or the campus police will arrest me for trespassing and the school will bring me up on additional violations.

Fortunately for me, three days later at the hearing, the guy who threw the flaming roll admits what he did. I am thrilled this ordeal is over.

Despite the resolution, I found that situation overwhelming. I felt completely alone. I had no understanding of what was going on and no one to guide me. The school or the cops could have explained it to me, but they didn't. I didn't know what I was charged with or how this was going to affect me and my future. I knew I had the right to remain silent. But the cops didn't read me my rights, so I just started answering their questions without discretion when they came into the room. Every action I took felt like the wrong action, and I didn't know how to make it right. And this was for something I didn't even do!

WHY I WANT TO HELP YOU AND YOUR TEEN
I don't know if this incident is the only reason I went to law school, but I do know it made me want to fight for young people in similar

situations. I want kids to know they have options when they feel like they have none. Because often, it's not clear. Often, it's not even fair.

When I graduated law school, I got a job working as an assistant district attorney for the Nassau County District Attorney's Office. I prosecuted criminal offenses for a little more than three years until I felt confident that I knew enough to represent those same people I was prosecuting. I opened my own criminal defense practice on February 2, 1998. (Groundhog Day is now a big holiday in my family). Since then, I have represented young persons for all kinds of offenses in every type of venue you can imagine. I have represented juveniles in criminal court as well as in family/juvenile court; I've represented students aged 14 to 19 in high school disciplinary hearings; and I represent students accused of violating the code of conduct of their college, law school, medical school, dental school, graduate school, or doctoral program.

The most common phrase I hear from parents of the teens I represent is, "If I had only known." They believe that if they had had a greater understanding of the legal consequences of underage drinking or the dangers of social media or the school rules about academic misconduct, they would have been better able to guide their kids before they got into serious trouble.

I wrote this book because I have seen up close every way a kid can get in trouble. I want to give parents a peek behind the curtain, so they have the tools

- to explain to their kids what the legal process is really like,

- to understand the reality of what happens if their kid gets caught, and

- to know the steps they and their kid need to take if they ever find themselves involved with the law or their school.

Many parents believe that it is enough to simply tell their kids, "Stay out of trouble. Don't be stupid. Do the right thing." But I believe there's more to it. I believe that parents and their kids need to know what could happen *before* it happens so they can make smart decisions in the moment. Kids need to know how to handle themselves in certain situations, such as:

- What do you do if a police officer wants to ask you a question?

- What do you do if a friend wants to drive home drunk?

- What do you do if your friend wants to cheat using answers from your Organic Chem test?

- What if the guys in your fraternity throw a keg party that ends with a call for an ambulance?

I wish that every parent and every kid in trouble could know what I know so they wouldn't be so lost or scared, but they don't. And because they don't, I want to share as much knowledge as I can in the hopes that people will read this book and use it if they ever need it.

I'M NOT JUST A LAWYER—I'M A PARENT, TOO
I have two daughters.

I've been a working lawyer in the Long Island area for almost 30 years. I've been involved in criminal cases with teenagers both as a prosecutor and as a defense attorney. I know the ins and outs of the legal system and the risks that your kid faces when he uses a fake ID or gets caught smoking pot on campus or ordering a plagiarized paper from companies such as Chegg.com. However, those aren't the sole attributes that make me qualified to write this book.

As of this writing, my wife and I have two college-age daughters. From an early age, they understood that I helped people in trouble.

Not only would I speak to them about the issues I would deal with but, when watching a show like *iCarly* together, I would point out the various felonies the characters were committing by breaking into their teacher's home or some other "practical joke" they were playing on someone (I am a lot of fun at home, as you can see). iCarly felonies aside, I explained how people got in trouble and how speaking to the authorities might get them into even more trouble. They learned that if they were asked questions by someone, it was okay not to say anything, and that then they should ask to speak to their mother or father. And when they became old enough to be in situations where they were around alcohol or drugs, we had discussions about making good decisions.

I have no intention of telling you that you that you will be able to dissuade your kids if they are determined to drink or try marijuana. Likewise, I have no intention of telling you not to be scared and that it'll all be all right because you can trust that the police or the school will do the right thing and justice will win out. That's not always the reality.

What I can do is help you teach your kid to be smart. I can help you learn what the legal system is really like, what the challenges and the risks and the consequences are. And I can help you so that if that moment comes when your teen might be in trouble with the law, as I was, you won't be in the dark.

Know this: You and your child and your family are not alone. You are not powerless. This book is designed to help you when everything feels out of control. You and your teen have options. You have rights.

The legal and academic worlds may not always be just, but you and your teen *do* have a fighting chance. Always. Read on to find out how.

CHAPTER 1

Fake IDs

Sometimes teens consider getting a fake ID if they want to buy alcohol or go to a bar. About 12.5 percent of pre-college students and 32.2 percent of college students have admitted to possessing a fake ID; in 2020, there were 14,000 fake IDs seized in the city of Cincinnati alone.[1]

Today, fake IDs are ingrained in the American youth experience, but it wasn't always this way. The quick rise of fake IDs came when the drinking age was raised to 21. The National Minimum Drinking Age Act of 1984 forced states to enforce the new age restriction or risk losing 10 percent of their highway funding.[2] This led to more arrests and a more hardline stance on fake IDs.

For many parents, fake IDs are an awkward issue to discuss. How do you convince a teenager of the perils of having a fake ID and of underage drinking without feeling like a bit of a hypocrite? Perhaps you remember your own glory days as a 19-year-old, pounding shots at your local dive bar.

In this chapter, we'll explore the consequences for teens of getting caught with a fake ID. I'll give you some unhypocritical advice you can impart to help them stay out of serious trouble. Let's start with a few facts.

FACT #1: The majority of kids in the U.S. will drink before they turn 21. Translation: There is a good chance *your kids* will drink before they are 21.

FACT #2: If your kid drinks, she will most likely use a fake ID.

FACT #3: In all likelihood, your teen will not get caught using a fake ID.

When I was in college, I used a fake ID. Back then, New York State licenses were simple slips of paper on which, with a bit of creative penmanship, it was possible to convert a 1969 to a 1964. Like that, I went from 17 to 22. When the state switched to licenses with pictures, a similar-looking 21-year-old friend gave me his license. Simple as that, I was good to go.

But that was in the '80s and '90s. Since then, the laws have changed.

When I began my legal career as a prosecutor in the Nassau District Attorney's Office, I was appalled to find 19-year-old kids being brought in on felony forgery charges for using fake IDs. These kids were arrested, taken into custody, held overnight in a jail cell, and told they were facing a permanent conviction that would go on their criminal record. These young people were facing serious ramifications simply because they wanted to engage in a teenage rite of passage. While most cases were reduced or dismissed altogether, the stress for the teens and their families was very real.

Over the past two decades, New York State has seen a rising number of fake IDs confiscated and underage drinkers arrested. This trend can be attributed to a few factors:

- **Stricter laws to deter underage drinking.** New York's DMV now runs a program called "Operation Prevent," which sends police officers to venues, concerts, and events to target underage drinking. This is primarily a political move for publicity, but similar initiatives are appearing in other states as well.

- **A larger supply of fake IDs.** Easier access = More fake IDs = More arrests. Nowadays, kids can order fake IDs online for as little as $50 each. Watch out for popular websites such as IDGod and foreign distributors. Out of the 14,000 IDs confiscated from Cincinnati in 2020, 97 percent of those were shipped from either Hong Kong or China.[3]

• **Better technology to detect fraudulence.** With current technology, telling a real ID from a fake is as simple as downloading an app like Age ID, Scanner, or Vemos. No need for vigilant bouncers to shuffle through "the book" of state IDs any longer.

What will happen if your kid *does* get caught with a fake ID?

SCENARIO #1: Your kid is turned away by the bouncer and spends the night with a Domino's pizza, binge-watching TikTok. Luckily, this is *the most likely* scenario.

SCENARIO #2: The bouncer takes your kid's ID. At the end of the night, they toss it into a dingy desk drawer in the back, never to see the light of day again. Occasionally, bouncers or venue owners will turn the IDs into the cops to curry favor with the State Liquor Authority, but this is rare.

SCENARIO #3: Your kid's ID is seen by the cops, and your teen is charged with a violation of the Vehicle and Traffic Law. In New York, this can result in a $300 fine, 15 days in jail, and a license suspension of 90 days. Before you worry too much, first-time offenders almost never serve jail time. However, the fine and license suspension are all but guaranteed. You can try to contest the 90-day license suspension, but if you lose the case, your kid will face a 12-month license suspension instead.

SCENARIO #4: Your kid is caught by the police and charged with a violation of the Penal Law.

In New York, this can mean one of three things:

1. Your kid has a fake ID they bought online and is charged with criminal possession of a forged instrument. This is a class D felony, which could come with a prison sentence of two to seven years.

2. Your kid is "borrowing" an ID from someone older and is charged with criminal impersonation, which is a class A misdemeanor that could come with a year jail sentence, three years' probation, and a $1,000 fine.

3. Your kid is charged with Criminal Possession of a Forged Instrument in the Third Degree, which is also a class A misdemeanor.

SCENARIO #5: Your kid is pulled over by the police for a traffic violation. Instead of showing their real ID to the cop, they show their fake ID. (Believe it or not, this scenario is responsible for the majority of the fake ID cases that come through my door.) The kid, who may have simply been sent on his way with a speeding ticket if he'd showed his real ID, is brought into the precinct and charged for using a fake.

Most district attorneys in my area are reasonable when it comes to prosecuting fake ID cases. There is an understanding that most teenagers who commit this crime aren't malicious. They are young and made a mistake, so they deserve a conclusion to the case that will not have long-lasting repercussions. For that reason, the incident is rarely recorded on the teen's criminal record. That said, it isn't fun to spend months in court with anxiety hanging over your head.

WHAT I TELL MY DAUGHTERS
Now, let's operate under the very realistic assumption that scaring your kids out of using a fake ID will be an exercise in futility. When I

talk to my daughters about the risks and responsibilities of drinking, I am realistic about their desire for freedom and independence. Yet I want them to be safe. I tell them:

1. **See what the culture is like in your town.** In some towns, particularly those with a large student population, some of the finer drinking establishments will be happy to look the other way in order to get more business from underage drinkers. In other towns, however, they will be more than happy to make an example out of some cocky kid with a shoddy fake ID. For example, one of my daughters goes to college in a conservative Massachusetts town where she won't see the inside of a bar until she is 21. My other daughter lives in Hell's Kitchen in New York City. As long as she's got a decent fake ID, she can saunter into almost any bar and down beers with all the other 18-year-olds. Talk to the older students to gauge the situation in your area.

2. **Know the laws *in the state where you attend school*.** In New York, a fake ID might be a simple violation of Vehicle and Traffic Law. In Illinois, however, it could be considered a class 4 felony punishable by up to three years in prison and a fine of $25,000.

3. **If you use an older person's ID, at least make sure it's reasonable.** No, you cannot pass for your 34-year-old cousin.

4. **Don't be the doofus who doesn't know ALL the information on your fake ID.** Name, address, DOB, height, weight, all the way down to eye color.

5. **Only try to get into bars that have minimal technology.** That karaoke bar that allows you to show your college ID and get a drink? Go to that one.

6. **Don't carry your fake ID on you all the time.** You forget the fake is in your wallet and the next thing you know you have a pending criminal charge.

7. **But also, don't leave your fake ID in plain sight.** If you live on campus, RAs can enter your room. If they find a fake ID, they can legally confiscate it and report you for violating your school's Code of Ethical Conduct. This can result in a warning, probation, fines, or even suspension.

8. **Know the stats.** If you are going to drink illegally underage, then you should be aware of all the potential negatives. According to the U.S. Centers for Disease Control and Prevention (CDC), underage drinking is significantly correlated with poorer academic performance, increased suicide and homicide rates, and unplanned pregnancies.[4]

Parents: Review this basic list of strategies with your teens. They don't need to be saints to stay out of trouble; they just need a little common sense.

CHAPTER 2

Drinking at home

Teens drink. A lot.

According to a 2017 survey, 7.4 million minors in the U.S. had consumed alcohol in the previous 30 days and 4.5 million of those were binge drinkers (defined as consuming five or more drinks within a couple of hours).[5]

Based on these statistics, many parents want to educate their children by allowing them to drink at home. A glass of wine with dinner or a beer at a family barbecue can be a safer first drinking experience than, for instance, your daughter doing Jell-O shots at a house party where she doesn't know her tolerance and could find herself in a dangerous situation. (Better the devil you know, right?)

In many states, it is actually legal for underage drinkers to consume alcohol in their parents' presence with their parents' permission. That said, no state allows an adult to give alcohol to an unrelated minor, even on private property. Through Social Host laws, adults who host unrelated underage drinkers on their property can be held criminally or civilly liable. So, although you might permit *your teen* to drink, you should be cautious about letting your teen's friends drink at your house.

THE THREE RISKS

There are three risks of allowing underage consumption of alcohol in your home:

1. Criminal consequences

2. Civil consequences

3. Psychological and social consequences

The above consequences are unlikely to occur unless one of two things happens:

- A complaint (e.g., your neighbor calls the cops because the kids are blasting the Foo Fighters at 11 p.m.)

- A tragedy (e.g., an ambulance is called because your kid's friend thought the vodka punch tasted like juice and, eight cups later, had to have his stomach pumped).

That said, while consequences are unlikely, they aren't impossible.

Criminal Consequences
If you are caught allowing minors to drink on your property and you are arrested, you will be taken into custody and brought to a police station. Then a) you'll be released and given an appearance ticket requesting you come to court at a later date, or b) law enforcement will hold you overnight and bring you to court the next morning to be arraigned. Where I practice on Long Island, if you are convicted, it is $500 for the first offense. Most people are smart enough not to get caught twice but, if it happens, it can result in a fine of $1,000 and jail time.

It is easy to get arrested but hard to get convicted. To be arrested, all the police need is probable cause to believe you committed the offense. It is a relatively low bar. However, in a criminal case, you must be proven guilty of the offense beyond a reasonable doubt in order to be convicted. That is a very high standard to reach. For example, in "Nassau County," the law states that it is illegal for anyone over

"21" who owns or rents a home to "knowingly" allow minors to consume alcohol on the premises. The key word here is "knowingly." If you are arrested and the prosecution is not able to prove beyond a reasonable doubt that you knew minors were consuming alcohol on your property, then you will not be convicted.

Case in point:

In 2018, a parent in Suffolk County was acquitted of misdemeanor charges for violating Social Host laws.[6] His teen hosted a party that ended when a fellow student succumbed to alcohol poisoning. Since an ambulance was called to the scene, it was reported to the police and the parent was arrested. Although the parent had purportedly checked on the teens during the incident, he didn't investigate the basement, where the majority of drinking was taking place. The justice chose to acquit the parent because there was sufficient reasonable doubt that he was aware of the underage drinking in his household.

What action should you take if you DO become aware that your teen and his friends are drinking?
If you discover underage drinking, the law states you must take *corrective action*. That means taking steps to stop illegal activity on your premises. It can include confiscating the alcohol, ending the party, or even calling the cops.

What if you aren't home and your kid throws a party, and they get caught?
You and your underage child will not be arrested or convicted of criminal charges. However, you can be liable for a *civil penalty*.

What if your 16-year-old throws a party and your 19-year-old is watching TV upstairs and the police get called to the house? Could the 19-year-old be arrested for violating Social Host laws?
In Nassau County, anyone 21 years or older can be charged under the Social Host Law. But it is important to know the law where you

live. In neighboring Suffolk County, anyone 18 years or older can be charged; and in Garden City, a village in Nassau County, anyone over 16 can be charged.

Civil Consequences

Civil consequences are incurred when an accident happens as a result of underage drinking on your property. As a homeowner, you are liable for any damage that results from this activity. For example, suppose your teenage daughter throws a party while you are out of town. Your daughter's friend downs six tequila shots before coming to the party and one beer after arriving. Next, she gets in her car and crashes into your neighbor's yard, resulting in significant property damage and a hospital bill. You, as the homeowner, can be sued even though you weren't home at the time, you weren't aware of the underage drinking, and the majority of the alcohol was consumed prior to entering your premises.

This also applies to any house that is *rented* under your name. Say your kid rents a house in the Hamptons with a few friends for prom night. You agree to sign the rental agreement. You know and I know that they will not be there for a tea party (unless it's a Long Island Iced Tea party). If they party a little too hard and trash the rental home, *you* may be held responsible for the property damage because your name is on the agreement. Likewise, if they leave the home and cause damage somewhere in the surrounding area, you can also be held responsible.

Psychological and Social Consequences

For most people, the ordeal of getting arrested, hiring an attorney, and attending multiple court cases can be traumatizing. While the consequences of conviction may be minor, the psychological impact of this tribulation can be long-lasting. For instance, the aftermath of a public court appearance and news coverage, particularly if there is a tragedy involved, could also ultimately ruin your reputation, even if you aren't convicted. These stories spread like wildfire on parental blogs, social media, and throughout the school district. It is not only embarrassing, but it can impact your relationships with other families and affect your professional life.

You would be under not only public scrutiny but also self-scrutiny. Is a tragedy involving a teenager something you are willing to have on your conscience?

WHAT YOU SHOULD DO WHEN TEENS DRINK AT HOME

Personally, I'm not convinced that sending my kids off to college without exposure to alcohol is the best course of action. As someone who was drinking with his friends at 15 years old, I feel hypocritical telling my 20-year-old daughter not to have a bottle of wine with her friends at home. However, I am also a lawyer who is keenly aware of the legal ramifications, leaving me in a "damned if you do, damned if you don't" position.

WHAT I TELL MY DAUGHTERS

1. **Talk to your kids about drinking.** Once your kid reaches a certain age, it is time to address the ins and outs of alcohol:

   - What is a reasonable amount to drink, and of what specific drinks (beer, light beer, wine, wine cooler, hard liquor, etc.)?

   - What is a safe environment to drink in?

   - Whom should you drink with?

   - Reasons why should you never ever drive drunk.

While some parents avoid conversations like these because they don't want to encourage drinking, you should understand that your kids will likely drink. It is your responsibility to teach them to be safe.

2. **Talk to your kids in hypotheticals.** While you can't give your teen direct permission to drink with their friends in your home, you can say something like this: "You cannot have your friends over to drink. But hypothetically, if you did, how would you make sure you were doing it safely? How would you prevent your friends from driving home drunk and getting wrapped around a telephone pole at 3 a.m.?" Hypotheticals excuse you from direct "knowing," but also ensure you can have an honest and thorough conversation with your kid about the potential consequences of their actions and about your availability to discuss these issues in the future.

3. **If worse comes to worst, it's okay to call the cops.** I had a friend call me in tears, asking for my advice, because their kid threw a party with 50 teens and the drinking was getting out of control. Here's what I told my friend: "At this point, trying to confiscate alcohol from every teen will be impossible. You'll get two beers and then they'll crank the music back up. If you call the cops, you will not be held liable because you took corrective action. Your teen might hate you for a while but, hey, most teens hate their parents at some point! They'll get over it."

4. **Get good liability insurance.** You have a teenager. This is a good idea for more than one reason.

5. **Identify the responsibility of the host.** I have heard so many stories from my kids about parties they went to where the host of the party was the first to start drinking and the first to throw up and pass out. I understand the desire to have fun when you are hosting a party, but it must be looked at as a serious responsibility. Hosts should not allow anyone who attends the party to drive home unless they're sure the guest has **not** been drinking that evening. Alternate transportation should be arranged (for example, a designated driver or a taxi), and guests should be allowed to stay over instead of driving home.

While "knowing" too much may be risky when it comes to social hosting, knowing the laws and the consequences can ultimately save you from financial, emotional, and social damage.

CHAPTER 3

Driving while intoxicated

I t's the horror story everyone knows:

A 17-year-old kid goes to a graduation party and celebrates by downing one too many beers. At the end of the night, he decides he is fine to drive. But he's not. The evening doesn't end well, and he gets into a massive collision.

Maybe you heard this story during a boring gymnasium seminar in your own sophomore year. Maybe you saw it on your local news. Maybe you even knew a kid who died after a night of drinking with his buddies. We all know the story because, unfortunately, it is all too common.

I believe that America's harsher stance on intoxicated driving over the past few decades has been a positive change. When I was a kid, drunk driving wasn't as taboo as it is now. After years of unnecessary fatalities, our society now treats drunk driving with the seriousness it deserves. As a result of this changing perspective, between 2000 and 2009, it was reported that fatal crashes involving underage adults (aged 15 to 20) had declined by 35 percent.[7]

Talking to your teen about DUIs and DWIs is different from the other legal matters we've discussed, because this activity is completely unacceptable. It is not in the morally gray area. It is not something that can be planned for or mitigated. It is simply wrong. The worst-case scenario is not merely a fine or a court case or even jail time. The worst-case scenario is death.

Think this sounds dramatic? Here are a few cold, hard facts on drunk driving:

- According to the National Highway Traffic Safety Administration (NHTSA), 29 people per day die in the U.S. as a result of alcohol-impaired driving.[8]

- Drunk driving costs the U.S. $132 billion per year and $500 per tax-paying adult.[9]

- Of drivers aged 15-20 who were killed in fatal car crashes, 33 percent had a blood alcohol content (BAC) of 0.01 or higher and 28 percent had a BAC of 0.08 or higher.[10]

- The average drunk driver drove while intoxicated *80 times* before their first arrest.[11]

- 25 percent of all car crashes with teenagers involve an intoxicated minor.[12]

Now that we understand the impact of drunk driving, we'll explore the legal consequences of getting caught.

WHAT THE LAW SAYS
While every state is different, most follow a similar process. The following legal parameters are set up in New York. (Note: A general rule is that it takes three to four drinks within an hour to blow a .08 on a Breathalyzer test, but the person's age, weight and gender also factor into the equation.)

- Driving While Intoxicated (DWI): 0.08 Blood Alcohol Content (BAC) or higher or other evidence of intoxication

- Aggravated Driving While Intoxicated (Aggravated DWI): 0.18 BAC or higher

- Driving While Ability Impaired by Alcohol (DWAI/Alcohol): more than 0.05 but less than 0.07 BAC, or other evidence of impairment

- Driving While Ability Impaired by a Single Drug Other Than Alcohol (DWAI/Drug)

- Driving While Ability Impaired by a Combined Influence of Drugs or Alcohol (DWAI/Combination)

- Chemical Test Refusal: when a driver refuses to take a chemical test (normally a test of breath, blood, or urine)

- Zero Tolerance Law (when a driver who is less than 21 years of age drives with a 0.02 to 0.07 BAC)

In New York, if you are convicted of a DWAI, it is a non-criminal charge. It is a violation of the Vehicle and Traffic Law, meaning it would *not* go on your criminal record. It would, however, result in a 90-day license suspension, classes, a fine, and potentially up to 15 days in jail.

If you plead guilty to a DWI, on the other hand, it is considered a misdemeanor. You will have a permanent criminal record as well as a six-month license suspension, ignition interlock, a fine, classes, and maybe a leg brace that detects any time you drink alcohol, as well as the possibility of up to a year in jail.

And that's not all. If there were any extenuating circumstances such as an accident, injuries, minors present in the car, drugs found, or a BAC of 0.18 or higher, you may face more severe punishment and possible jail time. For example, if you hurt someone in an accident while under the influence, you could face four years in prison, in addition to your penalties for driving under the influence. If you injure more than one person, you will be charged with one count of vehicular assault for each person injured. With deaths caused while under the influence, charges are even more severe. DWI manslaughter charges can lead to a sentence of up to 15 years in prison.

Think you're better off bypassing the potential charges and *not* taking the breath test? In New York, as part of getting a driver license, you agree to take a breath test if asked by an officer. If you refuse, you not only raise the cop's suspicions, but you will automatically be slapped with a $500 fine and a year-long license suspension.

And if your 19-year-old decides to have one beer and gets behind the wheel, if she is pulled over and blows a 0.04 BAC, she would be charged with driving after having consumed alcohol. Instead of going to criminal court, there would be an administrative hearing. The result of this type of charge would most likely be a driver license suspension for at least six months, plus fines, as well as the offense remaining on your child's record for three years or until she turns 21, whichever is longer.

CONSEQUENCES
Let's review longer-term consequences of these charges.

- **Your teen will have a criminal record.** If they are convicted of a DWI misdemeanor, they will have a criminal record. This means that when an employer, a landlord, or a bank does a background check, they see that your child has a criminal conviction. They can lose out on lifelong opportunities simply for making a bad mistake at 19.

- **Your teen's insurance will go up.** *Way up.* In New York, the average insurance rate increase following a DUI/DWI conviction is 76 percent.[13] And this charge can impact your kid's car insurance for a full 10 years![14]

WHAT I TELL MY DAUGHTERS

I believe it's better to be realistic and expect that your kid will drink and teach her to be safe about it. How do you impress upon your kids the importance of not drinking and driving?

1. **Know the stats.** Beyond the ones I've mentioned, keep up to date with the latest stats on drinking and driving through the National Highway Traffic Safety Administration (NHTSA), Mothers Against Drunk Driving (MADD), and the Centers for Disease Control and Prevention (CDC). Part of responsibility is awareness.

2. **"Just a couple of blocks" is more than enough to get in trouble.** I once had a client who was convicted of a DWI because he was intoxicated, had stopped at a stoplight, and a bicyclist crashed into him. Since the cyclist was injured, the police and ambulance were called, and they arrested my client even though he was just sitting in his car at the light. The point is that even if you believe you're being careful, you can get stopped anywhere at any time and a DWI will come into play. Many of my clients have been stopped by a cop right in front of their houses. In the end, it doesn't matter if you're going two blocks or 20 miles. Cops could be anywhere. Accidents could happen anywhere.

3. **Reach out to me.** I tell my daughters that if they're ever in a situation where they are intoxicated and the options are to drive home or to stay in a place where they don't feel safe, always call me. It's better for me to be angry with them than for them to put themselves or someone else in danger.

4. **Your friend is not a "crazy-good drunk driver."** I tell them: "Your friend does not possess a special power whereby she is a better driver when she is drunk than when she is sober. What she does possess is alcohol-infused hubris." If you get in the car with her,

you enable her drunk driving, and you bear partial responsibility for whatever happens. No, you might not get charged if she gets pulled over and arrested for a DWI, but you chose to get in that car with her. You chose to help her put herself and you at risk.

5. **Have a good exit strategy.** When people are intoxicated, they quickly lose the ability to make good judgments. This is why it is important for teens to have a plan before they start drinking. Ask: "Will you be staying at your friend's house? If not, who will drive you home?" Don't rely on that last-minute Uber, Lyft, or a service through other ride sharing app, especially if you are under 18 and in a remote area. Know your plan of action before the bad judgment sets in.

6. **If you do get pulled over, cooperate.** Say your teen does drive drunk and gets pulled over. Tell him the best thing to do is to cooperate. Listen to instructions and try to speak as little as possible. Trust me, no one ever made their case better by speaking up. That said, he has no obligation to participate in the field sobriety tests. If he refuses, this fact could be used against him as consciousness of guilt, but there is no "implied consent" rule similar to the rule for the chemical tests.

7. **One stupid move could follow you around for the rest of your life.** Ask your teen: "Do you know what happens if you drive drunk, get in an accident, and one of your buddies in the car gets killed? You get arrested." His family blames you. You will forever be a villain to them, and you'll go through life knowing you killed someone. Whether your buddy was drunk or not. Whether you just drew the short straw and had to drive that night. You will still be blamed for your friend's death. If you're not prepared to carry that on your conscience for the rest of your life, don't get in the car.

When it comes to DUI/DWIs, the lesson is as simple: Tell your kids not to do it. EVER. You can be lenient about some things, but if your kid messes this up, they could face a lifetime of consequences.

CHAPTER 4

Cannabis

With the rising number of states legalizing marijuana, pot smoking is now at the forefront of many parents' concerns. I approach cannabis in a similar way to drinking: Whether or not you endorse it, there's a high (Dad pun intended) probability that your teen will try marijuana at some point.

Personally, I don't see marijuana legalization as a terrible evil. Yes, with changing regulations and the fact that pot is ubiquitous, kids these days *do* have easier access to marijuana. Plus, with the current popularity of vaping over smoking joints, it is easier than ever for kids to hide the smell. However, marijuana legalization has some benefits: it increases state income, takes power away from the illegal market, and may actually decrease marijuana use in underage populations.[15]

Benefits aside, marijuana is not risk-free. One study claimed that having cannabis in your system increases accident risk by 83 percent.[16] However, since pot can stay in your system for a long time, there is substantial debate as to whether marijuana use directly causes accidents or if use is correlated with other accident-prone behaviors. While pot is known to slow reaction time, its effects usually wear off within an hour.[17] More conclusive research is needed. For comparison, alcohol increases the risk of an accident by 2,200 percent.[18] So, while driving high on cannabis is not a good idea, it is not nearly as risky as driving drunk. Given the legal ramifications, as well as the increased risk, as a parent you should never endorse the car + marijuana mix.

LEGAL RISKS

Given the new laws, what are the legal risks of using cannabis?

Decriminalization does not mean zero legal consequences. When pot started to become decriminalized, people mistakenly equated that to mean, "Hooray! I can't be punished for smoking pot. Let's light up a joint right in front of this officer." What decriminalization actually means is that you won't face a criminal charge if you are caught with a small amount of pot. However, this doesn't prevent police from taking you into custody and issuing you an appearance ticket or, in some cases, holding you overnight to see the judge even though you will ultimately only receive a fine. Moreover, if you sell or if you have a lot of marijuana in your possession, you can still be criminally prosecuted in states where marijuana is decriminalized.

Even if cannabis is legal in your state, you must be 21 to use it. As of this writing, New York passed a law that states that personal possession of cannabis is no longer a crime. The law states:

> Adults aged 21 and older are allowed to possess up to 3 ounces (85 g) of cannabis flower, or 0.85 ounces (24 g) of concentrated cannabis. Public smoking of cannabis is allowed wherever cigarette smoking is permissible. Home cultivation of between 3 and 12 plants per household will be allowed. Possessing over 3 ounces could result in a top fine of $125. Possessing over 16 ounces is punishable with a misdemeanor. At their places of residence, people can possess up to 5 pounds or marijuana.

These facts represent quite a change. I had a number of very happy clients who were arrested on marijuana charges and, when the law changed, the charges were dismissed. But I think back on all the clients I have had over the past 23 years who were arrested for possession or smoking pot. And the ones I prosecuted before that for marijuana charges. I believe that marijuana is something that never should have been criminalized and I am glad it no longer is.

BUT—you still must be 21 to use. The question of how underage possession will be handled is unknown at this writing, but with New York's 62 counties, 932 towns, 62 cities, and 534 villages, I am sure it will be a jumbled mix, so you need to know the law in your area.

Low-Level Possession

This means that an officer finds only enough pot on a person to indicate personal use. Usually, this translates to 4 ounces or less. In many places in the U.S. where pot is decriminalized, the most serious charge first- and second-time offenders will face is a citation and possible detainment.

Selling

Selling, especially if your kid sells to other minors, is risky. This issue is exacerbated if school administrators or police catch your kid selling on school grounds. If caught, kids could face a year suspension from school and a proceeding in juvenile court. Your kid might think he's being entrepreneurial, but what he's actually doing is putting his entire future on the line for a few extra bucks from his buddies. And it just takes one of those kids to rat them out to the principal. It's never worth it.

Marijuana and Driving

It is challenging to prove in a court of law that someone was driving while high. Even if marijuana levels are measured on the spot, tolerance varies widely depending on frequency of use. Also, marijuana can be present in one's system for up to 90 days after smoking, so presence may not properly indicate intoxication. The officer pretty much has to see your teen smoking a joint or vaping while driving to pull them over and have sufficient evidence to arrest them.

That said, if your teen is pulled over for any infraction and the cop suspects that they have marijuana in their possession, the car will be searched. And usually, the pot is pretty easy to find. Most people keep it within reach while they are driving, so it's almost always in the center console, the glove compartment, or a backpack. And you can be sure that if it's in one of these usual spots, the police will search and then say that the pot was in plain view. Even if your kid hides the pot, the officer will search the car if he suspects pot is there, whether he has sufficient cause or not.

I had a case recently where a cop claimed that the car smelled like marijuana, and that he had found vaping cartridges to prove it. My first thought was, "How did the officer *smell* the pot? Vaping doesn't smell enough for that." The point is: If a cop wants to search your teen's car, he will find an excuse to do it and will find the pot. So, if your teens are going to smoke or vape, make sure they do their best not to drive with it in their cars.

One final point: Consider that being in a car with the engine running or even just the keys in the ignition can result in a DWI. This means that the kids hotboxing (that is, smoking in an unventilated area) in a Rite Aid parking lot at 2 a.m. with the engine on could be arrested for a DWI.

WHAT I TELL MY DAUGHTERS

Feel free to use this list to talk to your own teens about cannabis. I tell them:

1. **Know the risks.** If you're going to smoke, be aware of both the legal *and* health risks.

   According to the CDC, the likelihood of fatally overdosing on marijuana is practically nonexistent.[19] However, compiled research shows that marijuana use can lead to cognitive impairment, a greater risk of psychoses in adulthood, a higher incidence of illegal drug use, and an increased chance of cardiovascular disease.[20] And, although the risk is minimal in comparison to alcohol, marijuana actually leads to dependence issues in 1 out of 10 chronic users.[21] It's also important to know the distinction between smoking joints and vaping. While you are less likely to get in trouble with vaping, it contains a more concentrated dosage, meaning you may be more impaired after smoking. Not only that, but vaping is also correlated with incidents of severe lung damage[22] and a higher risk of contracting COVID-19.[23]

2. **Be aware of your surroundings.** Don't make it obvious. Don't smoke in your car in a sleepy suburban neighborhood with the lights on and the windows rolled up at 11 p.m. Or alone in a mall parking lot in the middle of the night. Or in the middle of a public park in broad daylight. Or on the front steps of your dormitory. Also, be sure to pay attention to the community. In some places, police will detain you for smoking pot because people want their suburban town to be Partridge-family friendly. In contrast, in a big city, you could be more brazen about smoking because there simply would never be enough cop cars to haul away every kid in the city who wanted to get high.

3. **Be responsible.** Even if your jurisdiction has announced that they will no longer be making marijuana arrests, this does not mean that they *can't* make arrests. If you provoke an officer, he will arrest you. In other words, if you're smoking a joint outside of a Taco Bell, and an officer comes by and you say, "I'm smoking pot, what are you gonna do about it, Officer?" Guess what? He can arrest you. Respect is essential. Just because pot is decriminalized doesn't give you license to be a jerk.

And, truthfully, that goes for any dealings anyone has with the police. If you act in an offensive way toward a cop, and he can't defuse the situation, there is a fair chance that he will arrest you for disorderly conduct. He knows that you won't be convicted because there won't be enough evidence, but that is not the motivation for that sort of arrest.

If you act that way toward a cop, his thought process will be, "You might beat the rap, but you won't beat the ride." Law enforcement sometimes refers to this as "contempt of cop."

At the same time, if you are questioned by a cop, don't implicate yourself. If you don't need to say something, then don't. As noted earlier, no one's case was ever made better by speaking up. There is only one circumstance in which you should speak to the police in this type of situation. If the police find pot in a car and no one takes responsibility, they might arrest everyone in the car based on the theory of *constructive possession.* This means that even though you may not have control over the item sitting on the floor of the car, the police could arrest all three people in the backseat and charge them with possession of the item. In that case, if the pot is yours, it is your responsibility to take the blame. Don't throw your friends under the bus for your mistake.

As I said at the start of this chapter, I personally believe that marijuana use is not an egregious offense. As a lawyer, I don't like making money defending a kid who decided to smoke half a joint in a golf course parking lot one night. That's why I want parents to help their kids be smart about marijuana use.

CHAPTER 5

Distracted driving

I magine this:

A 51-year-old New Jersey woman was driving when she received a simple text from her former sister-in-law about dinner plans in NYC: "Cuban, American, Mexican, pick one." Soon after receiving that text, the woman rear-ended another car at an intersection; that car then ran into a 39-year-old woman crossing the street. The pedestrian later died.

The NJ woman denied texting while driving, but the letters "M" and "E" in her text history tell a different story. The jury agreed with the evidence and sentenced the woman to five years in prison.[24]

This woman wasn't an evil person. In fact, she worked at a nonprofit agency that offered sustenance and health services for the homeless. She wasn't out to commit some heinous atrocity. But she did, simply because she wasn't paying attention.

WHAT IS RECKLESS DRIVING?

According to the National Highway Traffic Safety Administration (NHTSA), distracted driving is "any activity that diverts attention from driving, including talking or texting on your phone, eating and drinking, talking to people in your vehicle, fiddling with the stereo, entertainment or navigation system—anything that takes your attention away from the task of safe driving."[25]

With the rise of the digital age, distracted driving among teens is more common than ever. In fact, 12 percent of distracted drivers involved in fatal car accidents in 2019 were teens aged 15 to 19.[26] The most common cause of distracted driving in teens? Texting while driving.[27] A 2015 study of 101,397 teenagers in 35 states found that 38 percent reported texting while driving. Multiple studies show that texting not only slows reaction time but also decreases awareness and increases the chance of swerving.[28]

No one is immune to the potential tragedy of texting and driving. In 2011, a teen in Massachusetts was texting when he swerved into the opposite side of the road, colliding with another vehicle, and killing the driver; the teen received the maximum sentence for his inattention.[29] In 2020, in Fresno, police arrested a fellow police detective who was texting when he struck and killed a homeless man.[30]

Yes, the majority of people who text and drive are fine; however, I see the worst of what happens in these situations. This is not just a matter of getting a ticket; texting while driving can hurt people. The driver isn't intentionally *trying* to do something wrong. He's just trying to look at a meme or change the song on Spotify or respond to a friend about his date for prom. The next thing he knows, he's run through a stoplight and hit someone at a crosswalk.

LEGAL CONSEQUENCES OF RECKLESS DRIVING

Currently, 48 states and the District of Columbia ban texting while driving. Twenty states ban the use of handheld devices of any kind, and 38 states ban cellular use for new drivers.[31] In most incidents, a driver pulled over for distracted driving receives a citation and pays a small fine, between $20 and $500. However, this citation could have a severe impact on that person's driving record and insurance. In New York, for example, if an officer sees a cell phone anywhere near a driver's ear, they could be liable for a whopping five-point violation!

There are further penalties if the texting while driving violation involves an accident. If a person is injured or killed as a result of distracted driving, then the driver could face misdemeanor or even felony charges. And whether a severe or lenient punishment is imposed, the situation of accidentally killing a person due to distracted driving is *traumatizing*. I don't wish that experience on anyone.

That said, distracted driving is very difficult to prove in a court of law. What constitutes "distracted" is pretty ambiguous. For example, if you have a magnetic phone holder and you're using your finger to look at the upcoming streets on the GPS, is that considered "distracted?" What if you were changing the radio station just three inches below that? Unless, for example, your phone has recorded a text you were in the middle of typing while driving, it would be difficult for the court to indict you on these charges.

Consider also that the vehicle must be "in motion" in order to charge someone for distracted driving as a result of texting and driving. The definition of "in motion" can vary among states. Some states such as Texas, Florida, and New York actually *allow* texting at stoplights.

Here's the thing, though: this isn't a simple issue of legality. While 54 percent of all drivers admit to texting at stoplights,[32] consider that 50 percent of all car accidents happen at intersections,[33] and 55 percent of those accidents are due to driver inattention.[34] Texting at traffic lights decreases your awareness and impacts your reaction times, leading to a higher potential for collision.[35]

And that distraction doesn't stop at the stoplight. Just think how easy it is to start texting right before or after you've stopped. If you started a conversation at a stoplight, how easy is it to take a quick peek at your texts while you're on the highway for the next 15 minutes?

Luckily, many states, including New York, are introducing bills that prevent texting at stoplights.[36] And many states take preventative measures to dissuade us from distracted driving, such as phone monitoring for repeat offenders, implementing rigorous high-visibility enforcement efforts to catch people in the act, installing rumble strips to alert drivers veering off the road, and instituting Graduated Driver

Licensing that helps limit distractions by granting driving privileges incrementally for new drivers.

Tech companies are even on the safe-driving train. Apple introduced a "Do Not Disturb While Driving" feature. Developers introduced apps such as the Life360 Driver Protect Plan, which allows parents to monitor driving from their teen's cell phone, even indicating whether they are speeding.

WHAT I TELL MY DAUGHTERS

Personally, I don't think installing monitoring apps are the answer. At a certain point, you just have to trust your kids. Here's what I tell my daughters instead: **"Don't text and drive."** It's as simple as that. You may never get caught texting, but is it worth the risk of killing someone? Nothing is more important than being safe.

That said, I'll admit that there is a gray area when it comes to distracted driving. While texting is never a good idea, what about eating a granola bar? Talking over a Bluetooth hands-free device? Adjusting your GPS? These aren't terrible risks for experienced drivers. With my daughters, I implemented my own Graduated Driving Licensing Program that went something like this:

Step 1: No Unnecessary Distractions

When you are first driving, *everything* is a distraction. It's important that your teen become acclimated and comfortable with driving before introducing other distractions. While you might not have any problem putting onion rings on a burger while you are driving down the highway, the newly-licensed 17-year-old doing the same thing may spill ketchup on his pants and crash into the concrete divider while cleaning it off. For their first few months of driving, I had my daughters put their phones in the "Do Not Disturb" mode in the center console. We also agreed on no food, no friends, no GPS, and limited radio until they started to become comfortable.

Step 2: Introduce Distractions *Gradually*
Once my kids started getting more comfortable, they graduated to placing their phone face down on the passenger seat with the audio on so they could hear the GPS directions. Eventually, friends were allowed in the car (albeit quietly ... my younger daughter still tells her friends to shut up when they distract her). Encourage your kids to incorporate distractions only when they feel safe doing so.

Step 3: Drive with Distractions, but Carefully
By now, your teen should be aware that while having their phone on a magnetic holder is okay, they shouldn't be looking at it every 30 seconds. Nor should they, say, attempt eating a messy carne asada burrito while driving. Reassure your teen that, worse comes to worst, they can *always* pull over.

It is critical to instill in your teens the awful potential for tragedy that exists with distracted driving. They should avoid distractions not because they don't want to get in trouble, but because avoiding them is the right thing to do.

CHAPTER 6

How drivers should deal with the police

Dealing with the police can be terrifying no matter your age. You're driving your car, you see the red and blue lights in your rearview mirror, and suddenly your heart is going a mile a minute and your stomach drops into your shoes. Even if you've done nothing wrong, it's intimidating.

Once your child starts driving, there is a high likelihood that he will, at some point, have an interaction with the police. As a parent, it's important to have a conversation with your kids *before* that happens, so that they don't rely on their panic response when the cops pull them over. In this chapter, we'll address what drivers should do and how they should act and *react* when dealing with the police.

COMMON DRIVER-POLICE SCENARIOS AND HOW TO DEAL WITH THEM

Let's start by discussing two common scenarios kids (and adults) face and how to deal with them: traffic infractions and accidents.

Traffic Infractions

Tell your teen the following: "When you see that telltale red and blue in your rearview, here's what you should do."

1. Pull over to the side of the road once it is safe to do so.

2. Turn off your ignition and keep your hands on the steering wheel.

3. If it is nighttime, put on your interior light.

4. Do not get out of your car or move anything around; just wait for the officer to approach.

5. When asked for your license and registration, ask the officer if you may open your glove compartment to retrieve it (or wherever you keep that information).

6. Once the officer has that information, wait patiently while he runs your name for warrants and writes you a ticket or warning.

7. Drive away slowly and carefully. (Don't forget to signal when pulling out—no need to give the cop another reason to ticket you!)

8. FOLLOW ALL DIRECTIONS FROM THE OFFICER. Under no circumstance should you do anything to disobey his directions.

Accidents

This is obviously a more frightening scenario, which is likely to set off the "fight-or-flight" instinct. Do your best to ignore the instinct to flee. When you get in an accident, you have an obligation as a license holder to do certain things:

1. Exchange insurance and contact information with the other driver if there is physical damage.

2. If someone is hurt, you must not only exchange information, but you must call the police.

3. Do not, under any circumstance, leave the scene of the accident. A lawyer friend of mine represented a woman who hit
someone in a Home Depot parking lot. She called her father,
who was a cop, and he said, "Come home." She drove home
and picked up her dad and her uncle (also a cop) and returned
to the scene 10 minutes after the accident. The other cops
at the scene arrested her on sight for "leaving the scene of
an accident," a felony offense. Due to the seriousness of the
victim's injury, the woman wound up doing three months in
jail, not because she hit the person, but because she left the
scene after she hit her.

If you leave, cops assume that you are abandoning the scene
of the crime, especially if someone is injured. Even if you drive
only four blocks away out of panic or just around the corner to
call your parents, you can be held liable.

BASIC GUIDELINES FOR DRIVERS DEALING WITH THE POLICE

Tell your teen to follow these guidelines regardless of the situation.

Listen

If a cop gives you a direct request (i.e., "License and registration,
please."), you should comply. If he tells you to get out of the car, get
out of the car. If he tells you to get on the ground, get on the ground.
This is not a time for discussion or trying to reason with an officer.
There is no appropriate reaction other than compliance when you
receive a direct order from law enforcement.

Be Respectful

This should go without saying, but don't talk back. Don't ever call
the officer a derogatory name. Don't try to slip a cop a crisp new
$50 bill, thinking he'll let you mosey out of a speeding ticket. You'll
wind up with an attempted bribery charge. Most of all, *do not* have an

attitude. Even if you're tired or the cop is being unfair, it's never worth it. Remember, when a cop pulls you over, he is in control. Let him be and hopefully you'll get through the situation relatively unscathed.

Always Record If You Are Able
If you can, record any interaction you have with the police. The officer will then be less able to make false claims, especially when it comes to unlawful searches. That said, it can be difficult and come off as disrespectful to start recording as soon as the officer pulls you over. If a friend is present, commission him or her to be on subtle recording duty.

If you have an iPhone, you can use the "I'm getting pulled over" shortcut with Siri. Once you say those words to Siri, your iPhone will turn on the "Do Not Disturb" function of your phone, send your location to the designated contacts you set up, and begin recording video.

Another option is to download the American Civil Liberties Union's (ACLU's) Mobile Justice app, which allows the user to record video that will automatically be downloaded to a server. So, if the phone is destroyed, the video will not be.

As I said, whoever you are, talking to the police can be a scary ordeal. But I'd like to remind you that not every police officer will treat you badly. I happen to deal with the worst-case scenario situations, so be aware that this advice is simply to make those types of situations less likely for your teen.

LEARN HOW TO TALK TO COPS
Beyond listening, how should your kids respond to difficult questions if the cops pull them over?

People want to be helpful to cops. The police know this. They try to play on that natural inclination to get information from the person they are speaking to. For example, an officer may ask a few questions so he can evaluate whether a driver has been drinking or smoking. The police are trained to notice details that would lead them to this conclusion. Whether the person is guilty or not, the best rule of thumb is not to share any information that is not explicitly required in the situation.

But sometimes, it's not that easy.

While the safest course of action is to refuse to speak to the police even if you are an adult, not acceding to an officer's wishes can feel not only terrifying but next to impossible. So, let's talk about a few ways that teens can respond to common questions that cops might ask.

- **Do you know why I pulled you over?** In this scenario, you're walking a fine line; you don't want to admit you are wrong but playing dumb won't exactly endear you to the officer. If it's obvious what you did was wrong, and the crime is a minor infraction, I suggest being honest without being overly informative (i.e., say "I guess I was going a little fast," instead of "I was going 20 miles over the speed limit.").

- **Where are you coming from?/Where are you going?** Police ask these questions to get you talking so they can look for signs of impairment. You should give short, direct answers (e.g., "I'm driving home from my friend's house," or "I am going to the movies."). No need to give the history of your friendship with your buddy John or your thoughts on the newest *Avengers* film franchise. Remember: The more you talk, the more you can get in trouble.

- **Is there anything in your car I should know about?** When a young person has something in her car that she should not, and she is stopped by a police officer, it will probably be the most serious and stressful situation she's ever have had to deal with. She is trying to figure out the best course of action to avoid getting into trouble, and then the officer asks, "Is there anything in your car I should know about?" It's not only the answer that may be difficult, but often the young person's awkward reaction gives the officer the idea that something isn't quite right and might give them cause to ask additional questions to determine whether there is any contraband in the car.

- **Can I search your car?** Unless the officer has a warrant or evidence of criminal activity in plain view, he is technically not allowed to search your car without your permission. That said, if an officer wants to search your car, and if there is a trial at a later point, he will say you gave him permission or that the contraband was in plain view... and the jury will probably believe him. That's why, if possible, you shouldn't give the officer any reason to want to search your car. Be quiet and be cooperative. Do not make any actions that make you look like you are hiding something or potentially putting the officer in danger.

As a criminal defense attorney, I've instilled in my children at a young age the proper protocol should they be pulled over by an officer. Lucky for me, they haven't had to use my good advice. I hope the same will be true for your kids.

CHAPTER 7

Talking to the police

In the last chapter, we discussed how your child should talk to the cops if she is pulled over while driving, but what about talking to cops in other scenarios? What should a teen say if the police catch them at the scene of a crime and they are a suspect? What should they expect if they are brought to a police precinct? What should you do if the police show up at your door and you have no clue why they are there?

In this chapter, we'll cover the most important rule for talking to the police as well as tactics for dealing with the police in five specific scenarios:

1. Police show up at the scene of the crime

2. Police show up at a suspect's door

3. Police call on the phone

4. The ride to the precinct

5. At the precinct

These are universal rules for dealing with the police, so while I am giving you this advice to discuss with your kid, if you ever find *yourself* in a similar situation, you should follow the same guidelines.

First, let me restate the golden rule of talking to the police: *Keep your mouth shut.* If you and your teen get anything from this chapter, I hope it's this: *You have the right to remain silent.* Use that right. If you don't, then the likelihood that you'll inadvertently implicate yourself is high, no matter your intentions.

Don't make statements before consulting a lawyer. Having an attorney gives protection from the pressure to make a statement. Once an attorney tells law enforcement that a client has retained him, he can request that police stop questioning the suspect and, legally, the police must stop.

Now, let's talk about a few common scenarios where your teen might be questioned by the police.

Police Question You at the Scene of the Crime

It is so tempting in the moment to blurt out everything that happened during a crime to an officer of the law, especially when they approach you with a gruff, "What happened here?" Tell your teen not to talk to the police about what happened. In all reality, they will probably make the situation much worse for themselves. Take, for instance, this situation that actually happened to one of my clients:

There was a bar fight, and someone had his head busted open, but the police weren't sure who did it. (Keep in mind that a bar isn't the best place to get the most accurate information, considering that many people are intoxicated and it's dark and loud.) *When the police questioned my client at the scene, he told the police, "I was three feet away from him, but I didn't touch him!" My client thought he had exonerated himself by telling the police he hadn't hit anyone. Instead, what he did was put himself at the scene of a felony assault. He admitted to being three feet away from the victim, which was close enough for an attack. Together with recollections by other patrons, the police had probable cause to arrest my client.*

While the police might have enough evidence to arrest you without your admission, there is no reason to inadvertently help them gather more evidence. Once police decide to arrest you, there is no talking them out of it. While you may think you are being helpful or getting yourself out of trouble, you are actually providing the police with more fodder for prosecution.

Remember, parents, this applies to you too. If you are at the scene of the crime, any information *you* give the police could be used against your kid. Don't make the investigation against your child easier for the police.

Police Show Up at Your Door

It's 1 a.m. You hear a knock on the door. You go to answer it and see two police officers on your front porch. What do you do? If you're like most people, you'll open the door and ask the police why they are there. But once you open that door, you are basically inviting the officers into your home, to either search or to make an arrest. So, what do you do if the cops show up at your door?

Know that police **cannot legally enter your home** unless one of the following is true:

- A warrant has been signed by a judge.

- There are exigent circumstances (for instance, someone is in immediate physical danger).

- Police have a current view of criminal activity (for instance, there is a line of cocaine on your coffee table).

- Officers receive express permission from someone the police reasonably believe has authority to allow them to enter the house.

Although technically police are supposed to have your permission to enter, once you open your door, the report the cops complete will state that you voluntarily opened the door and invited them in (even if you didn't necessarily grant that permission). If you are worried that your teen (or you yourself) might be involved or potentially implicated in a crime, my advice is to talk to the police *through the door* without opening it.

If the police question you or your teen and ask for a statement, do not say anything until you have spoken with a lawyer. Likewise, if police ask your teen or you to go with them, do not accompany them anywhere, unless they officially place you under arrest. You are under *no* obligation to comply without an arrest.

The Police Call You on the Phone
If the police call and ask to speak to your kid, the rule is the same: *don't say anything.*

Often, they are calling to ask your teen to tell his side of the story and find out more details, or they are calling to ask him to come down to the precinct to give a statement. In the first case, your teen is under no obligation to give a statement or any information to law enforcement. The police are most likely trying to solicit information to assess whether they have probable cause make an arrest. They may already have enough evidence, but they may not. Making a statement at this point will either confirm the information they believe is true and/or provide them with information they did not know about. There is no reason anyone should ever speak to the police at this point as doing so can only help the police build their case.

In the second case, note that the police are *asking* the suspect to come to the precinct. Going down to the station of your own volition is *not* the same as being arrested and brought to the precinct. If you are arrested and accompanied to the precinct by the police, you cannot leave until the police release you. Alternatively, if the police request that you come and speak to them in person, it might seem like you are under arrest, but you aren't. You are free to leave at any time as long as they do not arrest you while you are there. Moreover, you are free to say "no" to their initial request to come down to the station.

That doesn't mean, however, that the police won't try to pressure you to come into the precinct. They'll act like you have no choice and use every buddy-up technique in the book to get you to come down to the station. In fact, it's possible they cannot make that arrest unless they have an admission from you, the accused. So don't give them the statement they need to arrest you.

In my role as an attorney, what usually happens in these situations is this: I get a call from a prospective client who is being told they must come in to talk to the police. I then call the precinct and tell the officer that I will be happy to surrender my client if they are making an arrest, but my client is not interested at this time in making a statement. If they have enough evidence to arrest my client, we'll set up a time when I will bring the client into the precinct. If they do not have enough evidence, the officer will take my information and then say that he will get back to me. Unless they obtain some other sort of evidence, they cannot move forward with the case.

The point: *Do not step foot in a police precinct without first consulting a lawyer.* It can save you a lot of frustration, a lot of angst, and a lot of heartache.

The Ride to the Precinct

Say your kid is arrested and a cop puts them in his car and drives to the precinct. The ride to the precinct is terrifying for anyone, let alone adolescents. They started the night out at a friend's party and ended it with an all-out brawl and an arrest. In their mind, they're probably thinking, "How the heck did this happen?"

The best recourse for a teen in this situation is, again, to just say nothing. Anything your kid says can and will be used against them. They should resist the overwhelming desire to ask the police questions and try to engage in conversation. Having the police officer think that your kid is just a regular guy caught in a bad situation may make him feel better in the moment, but it may be at the expense of giving the police information that helps their case.

At the Precinct

If your teen is at the precinct and is under arrest, it is because the police have probable cause or reasonable suspicion to make an arrest. My advice in this situation is exactly what I've reiterated through this chapter: *stay quiet*. Even if your kid is guilty. Even if your kid thinks the cops already know what happened. Even if your kid is innocent and has the texts to prove it. Now is *not* the time to talk. The interview and interrogation rooms at the precinct could be wired for sound and video and will record everything that happens while in that room.

Sharing a statement before consulting a lawyer never makes the situation better. Ever. As every single TV cop drama tells us, "Anything you say can and will be used against you in a court of law."

Yet staying quiet is easier said than done. Being arrested and waiting in a precinct is *terrifying*, especially for a kid. Most of them, at that point, simply want to go home to Mom and Dad. In fact, I've had clients who have been arrested and whom I've subsequently told never to make statements if they were ever in that situation again. Guess what? The next time they were arrested, they got back to the precinct and were so intimidated that they made a statement. *Again*. So, yes, it's challenging to keep your mouth shut, but remember: The police are scary, but conviction is scarier.

The same "don't tell" principle applies to giving up evidence prior to talking with a lawyer: *don't*. Many people are so anxious to tell their side of the story, especially if they think they can divert blame, that they share evidence prematurely and wind up giving the police more of a case against them. I had a client who, before hiring me, relinquished a videotape to the police of a fight he'd had with his girlfriend. He thought it would help him because it showed her being violent toward him. But it also showed not only that he was violent as well, but that he had *started* the fight. It ended up landing him in a lot worse trouble than if he hadn't shared the video.

Be advised: The police are trained in interrogation techniques to coerce people into giving up information. These techniques can be intimidating, comforting, or downright aggravating, and are all designed to break down people's defenses. Here are a few popular methods cops use to try to solicit a statement:

- **They play good cop/bad cop.** One cop perpetually seems on the edge of slamming your head into the table, while the other apologizes, saying his partner is just "having a bad day" and offers you Doritos and a Coke.

- **They make you wait in an uncomfortably cold room.** Trust me, the time waiting in a steel-backed chair in a room held at a chilly 60 degrees can feel interminable, especially when you're already a bundle of nerves.

- **They buddy up to you.** The cops say, "We'll put in a good word with the DA if you're honest with us," or "What happened? Tell us what happened today, and it'll be fine." It won't be fine. Remember, the police *are* allowed to lie to you. Even if it's absolute BS, they can say, "Well, we all get into fights sometimes. It's okay if you punched your friend, it happens to the best of us. He probably had it coming, right? You probably won't get in serious trouble if you tell us now." They will say what they need to say to get you to confess.

- **They tell the suspect that if he gives a statement, he'll get a Desk Appearance Ticket (DAT), so he doesn't have to spend the night in jail.** Many people will do almost anything to avoid going to jail, especially if it's their first time. They figure, "I'm already being arrested, I might as well tell them what happened so I can go home!" But often, after the statement, the officer says he "spoke to the supervisor" and did everything he could, but "you still have to spend the night in jail."

One additional note: With technology comes new issues. Often, when someone is arrested, the police want to look at the person's phone to see if any information there can provide evidence for the investigation. So, if your daughter is picked up, the police may want to see who she has called, what she's been texting, and where she has been. They may try to convince her to unlock the phone so they can look at it. But never agree to give them access by allowing them to open the phone with your fingerprint, face, or code.

My hope is that you or your teen are never in any of these situations. But if you are, I want you to recall what a law enforcement officer once told me: "Scott, just remember that cops tell their family never to give a statement to the police—there is a reason we give them that advice." So, tell your child that if she gets arrested, she should keep her mouth shut and call you as soon as they let her.

CHAPTER 8

What happens when someone gets arrested

When parents find out their kid has been arrested, their typical reaction is to be scared out of their minds. Rightfully so. I hope your teens never find themselves under arrest, but I want to give you the full picture of the process in case it happens.

It is critical to educate yourself and your teens on the criminal process *before* they have a run-in with the law. You never want to think your child could do something so wrong that the cops would arrest him, but it's not about that. He could be innocent, and the cops could still arrest him. His involvement in criminal activity could be completely accidental. Even the most well-behaved child could simply be in the wrong place at the wrong time.

That's why it's better to be prepared, even for parents who can't imagine their child getting in trouble. In this chapter, I'll walk you through the criminal process step-by-step:

Step 1: Arrest

Step 2: At the Precinct

Step 3: Arraignment

Step 4: The Criminal Case

Step 5: What Comes Next

STEP 1: ARREST

The definition of "arrest" is to seize someone and take him into custody. There are two ways someone can be taken into custody:

- **Immediate arrest.** This means the police have probable cause to arrest someone and the person is present at or found close to the scene. Imagine, for example, a 19-year-old gets pulled over for swerving into a highway divider. The police suspect him of being intoxicated and, sure enough, he blows a 0.09 BAC. Police arrest him on the spot.

- **Investigation and arrest.** This means the police investigate a crime, build sufficient evidence, and then look to make the arrest. This could happen in a matter of hours or months, depending on the nature of the offense. For example, imagine your neighbor calls the cops because the windshield of her Mercedes has been smashed and she suspects the 19-year-old boy across the street. When the police review your neighbor's front-porch camera, it shows the 19-year-old smashing a bat onto her windshield. The police then show up at the teen's door and ask him to come with them to the precinct.

If the police take your teen into custody, tell them there are certain guidelines they should always follow:

- **Be quiet.** As I have mentioned again and again, do not give a statement or any information pertaining to the crime, whether you are innocent or not.

- **Listen to what you are asked to do.** The golden rule of arrest is to *follow every instruction.* If the officer asks you to put your hands behind your back so he can put handcuffs on, you cannot reason with him. He is not interested in what you have to say. If you refuse or actively move your body in a way that shows you are not obeying the lawful orders of the police, the cops will charge you with resisting arrest and obstructing justice. Be quiet and follow the rules to the best of your ability. Generally, if you are nice to the officer, he will be nice to you.

Remember, if the police do arrest your kid, it is not the same as conviction. Breathe. Just because he is arrested doesn't mean he will have a record or go to jail.

STEP 2: AT THE PRECINCT
Once in custody, the police put the suspect in a squad car and drive him to a police station. After they arrive, they seat the suspect in a chair and possibly keep him handcuffed or handcuff him to the wall. From there, the police fill out paperwork, make a custody decision, and potentially allow a suspect to make a phone call.

The Paperwork
While filling out paperwork, the process will include:

- Pedigree questions, such as full legal name, address, etc.

- Questions about current physical and mental health

- Fingerprints

- Mugshot

- Waiting for the State Fingerprint Report to come back before police make a custody decision

The Custody Decision

When police decide whether or not to hold a suspect in custody, they have two options:

- **They issue a Desk Appearance Ticket (DAT),** which tells the suspect to appear in court on a given date. This happens in cases involving lower-level crimes, or when the suspect has no priors and there is not an immediate need to see the judge. This process will most likely take two to three hours.

- **They hold the suspect to see a judge at the court's earliest availability.** Police will hold suspects for more serious charges, particularly those involving violence. If the suspect is held, he typically spends the night in jail and sees a judge in the morning. However, if the suspect is arrested somewhere like New York City, where courts are open until 1 a.m., the judge might see a suspected perpetrator on the same day.

The Phone Call

The police are under *no obligation to inform you* that they are arresting your minor child. They can arrest her, bring her to the precinct, question her, and then at some point they may let her call you. *That is correct:* As the parent, you have no right to be part of this process. The police also have no obligation to tell you anything about what is happening. As a result, the call usually comes from the child after police have questioned her and processing has begun.

Parents: If you ever receive that call, this is what you should do:

- **Tell your kid not to make a statement.** If you're a parent, it's tempting to want to tell your kid to be honest, but this is the worst thing she can do in the moment. Instead, advise your kid to tell the officer something like, "I'm sorry, I know you're saying it'll help me to give a statement, but I need to talk with a lawyer before I say anything." Note that it may be too late by the time your kid calls you, in which case just tell her not to make any further statements and not to discuss the facts of what happened with anyone.

- **Ask your kid what she's charged with.** The police have no obligation to tell your teen what she is charged with, so she may be 100 percent in the dark. That said, any information is helpful.

- **Find your kid a lawyer ASAP.** Armed with whatever information you have, get your kid representation to help guide you and her through the process. Trust me, the BEST thing you can do is to hire someone like me right away. When the police are involved, you and your teen need an expert to guide you through the intricacies of the system.

If the police are holding your child to see the judge, then when they are done with all the paperwork and other required tasks, your child will most likely be placed in a holding cell until they are ready to be transported. Then at some point they will be transferred to either "central booking," which may be at police headquarters or attached to the courthouse, or they may be brought straight to the courthouse. Once at the courthouse, they will wait in a holding cell until the case is calendared by the court. Once the case is court-ready, your child will be brought into court for an arraignment, which is when the case turns from a police matter into a criminal court matter.

STEP 3: ARRAIGNMENT

After the events at the precinct comes the arraignment. The arraignment is when the court officially charges a suspect with an offense. Whether held overnight or given a DAT, the process described in this section is the same.

The Client Pleads "Not Guilty."

Why "not guilty"? What if a suspect did commit the crime? Shouldn't he be honest and plead guilty? While you may feel like it is the right thing to do, not only shouldn't your kid do it, but the judge will most likely *not allow* him to plead guilty. The majority of cases end in a plea bargain. If you plead guilty from the get-go, a suspect doesn't have the opportunity to seek a reduced charge or negotiate the punishment. Just because your teen committed a crime doesn't mean the DA's office won't be willing to work out a deal so that one stupid act doesn't hurt him for the rest of his life.

For example, in New York State, any property damage above $250 is considered a felony. So, think back to that 19-year-old kid from the beginning of this chapter who *did* smash the windshield of his neighbor's Mercedes. If he pleads guilty at the start, he could get a criminal record. But if he pleads not guilty and has a good criminal defense attorney, the goal would be to get the court to release him and find a non-criminal resolution involving restitution, anger management classes, and community service.

The Judge Makes a Custody Decision

The judge must decide the suspect's custody status while the criminal case is pending. The determination is based on the suspect's likelihood of coming back to court, her personal circumstances, and the nature of the charges. Judges have a number of options when it comes to custody:

- **Release on own recognizance (ROR).** The judge imposes no restrictions and believes the defendant is not a flight risk.

- **Release to a monitoring organization.** The judge releases the defendant, but she must check in with a pretrial release service, usually after court and or on a weekly basis.

- **Bail.** Bail can be set a number of ways:

  Cash Bail: A judge sets an amount of money that someone must pay in order to release the defendant.

  Bail Bond: A bond company will post a suspect's bond if she pays them a fee and provides collateral.

  Partially Secured Bond: The court will ask for up to 10 percent of the amount of the bond, and the surety promises to pay the full amount if the defendant does not return to court.

  Unsecured Bond: The person promises to pay the full amount if the defendant doesn't return to court but does not pay any money up front.

- **Deny bail and keep the suspect in custody.** This may happen for more serious offenses.

Request for an Order of Protection

If there is a victim in the case who has been harassed or assaulted, the District Attorney's office will almost always ask for an **Order of Protection** to protect the victim. There are two Order of Protection variations:

The Stay Away: This directs the defendant to stay away from the complainant at all times and not communicate with them in any way, either directly or indirectly, such as via electronic means or a third party.

The Do Not Harass: This allows the defendant and complainant to be together, but if the defendant harasses or assaults the complainant, then it would be considered a violation of the order.

If the defendant and complainant share children, the criminal court will *not* decide who gets custody of or visitation with the children. What the court will do is make the criminal court order subject to the order of the family court, which deals with custody, visitation, drop off, parent-teacher conferences, and other situations where the parental parties may come into contact.

At the conclusion of the arraignment, the judge will tell the defendant what date to be back in court for his next appearance.

STEP 4: THE CRIMINAL CASE

Remember: Arrest is *not* the same as conviction. It's relatively easy to be arrested. The standard is that the police must have "probable cause" to believe your kid committed a crime. It is a reasonably easy standard to meet. But once in court, to be found guilty of a criminal offense, the judge or jury must find the defendant guilty beyond a reasonable doubt. That is not such an easy standard to meet. I've had plenty of clients who were arrested for serious felonies who, at the end of the case, did not have a criminal record. I say this because, by this point in the process, both you and your child are *stressed*. It is so important to ground yourself in the reality that the worst will probably not happen.

Once retained, I evaluate the case. I ask myself: How strong is my case? What kind of case does the prosecutor have? What can she prove beyond a reasonable doubt? If there were a jury, what would they think about this fact or that fact? Most of the time, my goal is to work out a plea bargain with the DA's office so that 1) my client doesn't have a permanent criminal record, and 2) my client doesn't have to serve jail time.

There are two main arguments that I put forth to the prosecutor to get a favorable resolution for my client:

1. **We look at the facts of the case.** While there was enough evidence to arrest my client, does the prosecutor have enough evidence to prove my client guilty beyond a reasonable doubt? Are the witnesses intoxicated or otherwise impaired? Has the

complainant recanted their allegations? Did the police officer make conflicting statements about what he observed? These are all good factors for me to use when negotiating with a prosecutor or trying to prove my case to the jury.

2. **We look at the client.** What kind of person is my client? An 18-year-old on his way to State U to be a business major? A 22-year-old med student? A 20-year-old working a full-time job and volunteering at the local fire department? Hopefully I can say the client has never been in trouble. I will use any information available to show the prosecutor that my client is an upstanding citizen and a decent human being. I want the prosecutor to understand that if my client has a conviction on his record because of one really bad decision, he will have an uphill battle to climb his whole life. Does he really deserve that?

Often, the DA's office will agree, and we can come to a reasonably quick resolution. But sometimes it takes longer. Maybe they don't agree that the evidence is weak, or they believe they have a good case and, with what their witnesses have told them, they don't believe my client is a good guy. They think he is someone who deserves to be punished. If that is the case, or if the client refuses their proposed offer, then the case will move forward to trial.

The closer the case moves toward trial, the more prepared and familiar the prosecutor becomes with the case. Often, as prosecutors call in their witnesses to prepare for trial or review the paperwork in more detail, they realize they have problems with some aspects of their case. So, even though the case is on a path to trial, the prosecutor may make a new offer at any time. There have been many times that, on the Friday before or the Monday morning of the first day of a trial, the DA's office extends my client a new plea offer.

So, what happens if a client is found guilty? These are the possible penalties:

- **A permanent criminal record.** For a felony or misdemeanor, that may be expunged in certain circumstances.

- **Jail time.** For local prisons, this usually does not extend beyond a year or two.

- **Prison.** This is for serious crimes that necessitate serving more than a year behind bars.

- **Probation.** The client will be monitored, but not held, for a period of time.

- **Restitution.** Financial compensation to the victim for damages or injury.

- **Community service.** This is for less serious offenses and can range from volunteering at the local food bank to picking up trash on the side of the highway.

- **Evaluation, therapy, rehab, or classes.** These penalties are directly focused on rehabilitation. So, if your child was charged with getting into a bar fight, the DA might propose anger management therapy. If your child was caught shoplifting a Nintendo system, the DA might propose a five-hour "StopLift" class (yes, this is a real thing).

STEP 5: WHAT COMES NEXT

After the case is over, what permanent ramifications will it have for your child? I will discuss criminal records in Chapter 20, but for now I will cover a topic that comes up with many clients.

Many times, the client and his family are upset with the party who brought the charges. They feel that the complainant lied to manipulate the police into making the arrest and they want to sue the complainant for anything they can: libel, slander, intentional infliction of emotional distress, etc. Some of my clients believe they could be handsomely compensated if they got the amount of money equal to the pain they endured through the process of arrest and court.

It is my job to quickly bring them back to earth by letting them know two things:

1. **The party you are suing must have assets that are recoverable if you win.** Say, for example, my client's family wants to sue my client's ex-girlfriend for lying to the police about domestic abuse. The fact that she lives with her parents, works at Starbucks, and has $137 in her bank account probably doesn't make her a good candidate for recoverable assets.

2. **Attorneys will not represent clients on a contingent fee when there is little or no hope of recovery.** While I do not do this type of work, many clients say to me, "I will hire an attorney and they can take one-third of the fee we recover." Well, if the attorney puts in hours of writing a summons, filing complaints, and doing depositions, they do not want to get $45 for their efforts. Most attorneys want to know there is a good chance of recovery, or they will expect to be paid their hourly rate.

If these two factors are not an issue, there *are* cases where a civil suit is reasonable against a complainant. (Note: Here, I am *not* discussing the validity of suing law enforcement, which is a completely different issue.)

As hard as it may be for them, in most cases I tell my clients that they need to try to get past the situation on their own, with the help and support of their loved ones. I'm sorry to say that retribution or acknowledgment of wrongdoing by the other party will most likely never come. It feels terrible. No one likes someone to get one over on them. Human nature is to respond, to react, and to fight for what is right. But the sad truth is that most of the time, it is a futile gesture that leaves my clients feeling unsatisfied and resentful. After any criminal ordeal, my advice is simply this: *focus on healing.* In healing, you and your family can find the strength to move forward.

CHAPTER 9

Juvenile court

Make no mistake: there is a big difference between a 15-year-old and a 19-year-old being arrested for the same offense. If a 19-year-old shoplifts $250 worth of eye shadow and lip liner from Sephora, the cops will arrest her, and the case will go to criminal court. If a 15-year-old is charged with the same crime, her case will be heard in juvenile court.

In this chapter, we'll explore what qualifies a minor for juvenile court, what to expect if your teen's case goes in front of the court, and how the juvenile court system compares to the adult criminal court system. In New York, these types of cases are heard in "family court" but many states refer to these courts as "juvenile courts," which I think is more descriptive, so I will use that term here.

THE AGE OF PROSECUTION AND CRIMINAL RESPONSIBILITY

What does the court mean by a "minor"? Most states do *not* have a minimum age for prosecution. For the states that *do*, it can be as old as 12 or as young as 6. In New York, the age of prosecution is currently **7 years old**. (At the time of this writing, the New York State Legislature has passed a justice reform bill that raises that age to 12. The bill is awaiting the governor's signature.) Though relatively rare, arresting and convicting a young child is possible.

In most states, if you're under 18, the courts will not prosecute you as an *adult*. This is important, because if the courts convict you as a minor, it will not go on your criminal record. It used to be that if you were 16 or 17 in New York, the criminal court would hear your case. But, unfortunately, being "tough on crime" doesn't have the intended deterrent effect, especially when it comes to juveniles. What it does is punish those who need the most intervention and help. That's why, fortunately, a recent movement led to a change in the law known as the Raise the Age Act, which enacted a policy to raise the age of criminal responsibility from 16 to 18.[37] Now, unless a juvenile commits a truly heinous crime (such as rape or large-scale threats of violence), the courts charge him as a minor. In my opinion, this is the way it should always have been.

ARREST OF A MINOR

Usually, the arrest of a minor will follow most of the same procedures as the arrest of an adult. The minor will be brought to the police precinct. There, the police will do some paperwork and determine if he will be released or transported to a juvenile detention facility, where he will soon see a judge for arraignment.

It is possible that the police may seek to take a statement from a minor child. Every time I represent a minor and the police take a statement, the parents ask, "How can they question my child without a parent present? Why didn't they contact me?" Well, as noted earlier, the police don't contact parents because they know there is a good chance the parent won't let the child answer any questions; then the police may not get the statement they need. More importantly, again, there is no requirement for police to notify parents that they want to take a statement from their child.

Similarly, as when adults are questioned and lied to or promised leniency or a Desk Appearance Ticket versus spending the night in jail, the police are allowed to use these tactics to elicit a statement from a minor. As of this writing, Illinois just passed a law and became the first state to make it illegal for law enforcement officers to lie or make false promises about a case or custody to induce a minor to make a statement. It is a great start, and I can only hope that other states do the same.

THE PRE-COURT PROCESS

So, what happens after the cops arrest your minor child?

As in adult cases, after arrest, a juvenile receives either a Desk Appearance Ticket (DAT) for a future date or is held in custody at a juvenile detention center until a judge can arraign him. If held in custody, he will see a judge within 24 hours. The judge then determines if the juvenile should be released or should stay in a juvenile facility pending the case.

Where I practice, if you are given a DAT, then your first appearance will not be with the court, but with the probation office. I accompany the parent and child to the appearance with probation services and instruct them to bring the child's birth certificate and other identifying information. From there, the parents fill out forms about the child's education, personality, prior legal problems, etc.

If the charge is not serious, the probation office determines whether there is an alternative education or rehabilitative program that would be helpful to the juvenile. This is called "Adjustment." Where I practice, there is a wonderful program called the Nassau County Youth Court. The juvenile goes to this court and has an opportunity to explain why he did what he did to a jury of his peers who have gone through the same process. The jury deliberates and then issues a sentence, which usually consists of community service, educational classes, and future sessions as a juror in this youth court. Through this process, kids become familiar with the gravitas of the adult criminal process without suffering the adult consequences. This is probably the best program I have had clients go through. In a system that generally focuses on punishment more than rehabilitation, I feel the Nassau County Youth Court lives up to the intention of helping youth offenders truly understand their actions and grow as people.

In fact, for nonviolent and less serious cases, the juvenile courts generally recommend programs like these, which focus more on helping to address the underlying issues that led to the crime. Rehabilitative programs such as community service, drug or alcohol counseling, anger management, and various other workshops and programs are aimed at deterring future criminal activity.

However, if a case involves violence, or is a serious felony, or the teen has multiple priors, the probation office files a petition along with a deposition describing what happened with the court and gives your teen a date to appear before the judge.

IN JUVENILE COURT

Now, what happens if your kid's case *does* go to juvenile court?

For a family that has never gone through this process, juvenile court is stressful, concerning, and downright scary. *Just imagine it*: going to court, standing in line, going through metal detectors, waiting in a busy hallway for the court to call your case so you can be in a room with armed court officers and a judge looking down on you from an elevated bench. This is an atmosphere and experience that is truly jarring for most parents and teens, who probably thought they would never be in such a situation.

While the process can be overwhelming, what parents have to remember is that because you are in juvenile court, whatever the results of the case, even conviction, there will be no permanent searchable record of the offense. No fingerprints, no name in the database, nothing. Typically, if a case goes to juvenile court, there are only four options available to the judge and, as far as I see it, only one of those options is completely unacceptable to most clients.

Option 1: Adjournment in Contemplation of Dismissal (ACD). This means that the court adjourns the case to a date in the future. If your child does not get arrested during the adjournment period, the court dismisses the case at the end of that period. Other than an outright dismissal or a win at trial, an ACD is the best result.

Option 2: Conditional Discharge. The court discharges your teen's case, but your kid has to abide by conditions for a certain period of time. If she violates these regulations, the court can file a Violation of the Conditional Discharge and then the court can sentence your teen to a more serious punishment.

Option 3: Probation. With probation, your teen will have to follow rules and regulations, regularly check in with a probation officer, and be extra careful not to get himself in trouble again. It is *stressful* to follow the directions of the probation officer, knowing that if he gets in trouble again. he may violate probation and wind up in more trouble. But it will always be better than the alternative of juvenile detention.

Option 4: Placement in a Juvenile Detention Facility. This is the only unacceptable result for most clients. The other punishments in juvenile court are mostly rehabilitative. However, while juvenile detention facilities say they also have the goal of being rehabilitative, the reality is that they are not. In my experience, the clients who went to juvenile detention centers have not been helped in any way. They were just punished and exposed to the gangs, drugs, and violence that exist in most facilities. This is a place you never want your child to be.

It's important to note that dealing with juvenile cases in court can be more challenging than dealing with criminal cases in court. Believe it or not, the process to negotiate a plea is *easier* in a criminal case.

In an adult case, I'm working directly with the prosecutor and judge to reach a compromise. Usually, the prosecutor and I negotiate until we have agreed upon a plea offer. We then run it past the judge for his approval on the plea and the sentence. I then explain to the client exactly what the prosecutor proposed and what the judge agreed to as a sentence. By contrast, in a juvenile case in New York, the judge is in no way obligated to tell me what the sentence is before we enter into a disposition. I negotiate with the prosecutor for a plea deal, which we then submit to the judge. Then, independently, the judge determines punishment. There is no conversation.

In a criminal case, I know that at the end of the day, if it's not going my way, I can always take my best shot and try to convince one of the jurors that the prosecution hasn't proven its case beyond a reasonable doubt. In juvenile court, I don't really have this option. There are only "bench trials" in juvenile court, meaning there are no jurors. The judge hears all the evidence and makes the decision alone. That said, in my experience no judge will incarcerate a child unless the judge truly feels that all other options have been exhausted or that the child has committed an unspeakably horrific crime. It is the *last resort*.

Note that these experiences are specific to the counties in which I practice. It is certainly possible that what would be a relatively innocuous offense in my geographical region could be a serious offense in another region of the state or another part of the country. While a crime in one court might result in a simple plea bargain with some rehabilitative classes, the same charge in a different court could result in juvenile detention!

A FINAL NOTE TO PARENTS

As a parent and as a lawyer, I know how awful it is to see your kid get arrested and go to court, especially if it is the first time. Rest assured that in juvenile court, there is more of an emphasis on parental involvement, as a parent will be *required* to attend court with the child.

Juvenile court is never good, but if you're prepared, it may not be a nightmare. Educate yourself and your teen. I hope the day never comes when you need to apply this knowledge, but if it does, you'll know what to expect.

CHAPTER 10

Student rights in school

I magine this scenario:

The high school principal calls a junior into her office and accuses him of vaping weed in the school parking lot and sharing it with his classmates. She rifles through his backpack on the spot and, sure enough, she finds a vape pen.

The principal asks the student to confess and give up the names of the students who were smoking with him. She says that if he doesn't, he will get a more serious punishment.

Was what she did legal? What should the student do in response? Say nothing? Ask to call his parents? Be truthful and hope everything turns out okay?

When it comes to illegal activity, dealing with school officials is an entirely different ballgame from dealing with law enforcement. With law enforcement, you have certain constitutional rights, such as the right to remain silent and the right to be free from illegal searches. But courts give wide latitude to schools to determine their discipline policies. The courts believe that the need to maintain discipline in a school outweighs the privacy rights of the student. The moment your child enters school property, he is subject to the disciplinary rules of that school district. The school can search him. The school can question him.

As a parent, I think it is just as important to teach your kids about their rights and how to handle themselves with school authorities as it is to teach them about what to do when dealing with the police. So in this chapter, we'll focus on three areas of the law in schools that you and your teen should know about: search rights, interrogation, and drugs.

SEARCH RIGHTS

Typically, when a student is found in possession of an illegal item, such as drugs or weapons, the first thing parents say is, "The school searched him illegally! They violated my kid's rights!"

Well, I've got some bad news for you: There are no illegal searches on school property. Your teen's locker is not private; it's school property. Her backpack or purse isn't personal property that the school can't search. When anyone sets foot on school property, they are agreeing to the school's policies. Often, these policies allow for search of not only school property but everything on school property as well: persons, bags, and even vehicles parked on campus!

An example of how this can go awry: One of my clients, a high school student, was found in school with a vape. The school then decided to search his car, which was parked on campus. In the car, the school officials found a knife and charged my client with illegal possession of a weapon. This "knife" was actually a pair of flower clippers tucked away in a florist's apron that he had thrown in the back of his car. (His dad owned a flower business, where the teen worked.)

Although the school officials obviously drew the wrong conclusion, their search wasn't illegal, because my client's car was parked *on campus*. In the same vein, the principal from the beginning of this chapter wouldn't be wrong in searching the student's bag for a vape pen. The lesson here is to tell your teen to be *very careful* what he brings to campus. By being on school grounds, he voids his right to be free from the search and seizure of property.

Technically, school officials *do* need to have reasonable suspicion to search a student's belongings or person. However, "reasonable suspicion" could entail something as simple as the smell of marijuana on a student or even a rumor that there are drugs in the school. Reasonable suspicion is an easy standard to meet. But, in my experience, most schools won't target a student unless there really is sufficient reason to suspect the student's involvement in illegal activity.

INTERROGATION

If you're a true-crime aficionado, you are probably familiar with the Miranda Rights, that is: "You have the right to remain silent. Anything you say can and will be used against you in a court of law. You have the right to an attorney. If you cannot afford an attorney, one will be provided for you."[38] The police are only required to give a Miranda warning if two conditions exist: 1) they intend to question the suspect, and 2) the suspect is in custody.

So, do these rights apply to school campuses? No, they do not. Law enforcement needs to issue Miranda warnings only if you are in their custody and being questioned by them.

If a school official decides to question your teen, Miranda does not apply, because the school official is not a member of law enforcement, and the teen is not in police custody. The only occasion when Miranda may apply in a school setting is when a school resource officer (SRO), who works for the police department, conducts the investigation, or if the police ask the school to question the student, as the SRO or the questioner may be deemed an agent of the police. Further, other basic constitutional rights such as the right to remain silent, to free speech, to freedom of the press, and to be free from searches conducted without a warrant are restricted in a school setting. Courts hold that administrators fill a "parental" role while school is in session, thus negating the "need" for upholding these rights on school premises.

Since schools don't need to issue a Miranda warning or adhere to these other rights, students suspected of an infraction may find themselves in a room with an administrator who makes accusations, conducts a search, and demands a confession. Such was the case with the high school junior and principal mentioned earlier in this chapter. The principal was completely within her rights to search and interrogate the student suspected of vaping.

Now, it is important to note that because students are not tech-nically in custody, they can leave the principal's office at any time. They also are not required to answer any administrator's questions. But, for most students, this is a pretty intimidating situation. Do you remember being 16? It is not easy to look an angry assistant principal in the eye and tell him that you choose to remain silent and that you are going to leave the office.

While a kid might not be able to convince a teacher or principal that he has the right to leave the room at any time, it's important to make your child aware that he doesn't have an *obligation* to make a statement. Assure him that, while it might be scary and awkward, he does have a modicum of control in that situation. He *always* has the right to request that he speak with his parent(s) before talking further. So, while that principal is within her rights to question the high school junior, the student also has every right to keep quiet and request to call his mom.

A few years ago, I found out that many school administrators are now trained in the Reid Interrogation Method, which is used by the police to solicit confessions. *That's right*: School officials and administrators take a three-hour program to learn how to interrogate *like the police*.[39] That means that if an administrator pulls a student into his office to question him about an incident, using his Reid training, he will treat that student as if he is already guilty and employ police-tested techniques such as:

- Observation of nonverbal cues that could indicate lying. (Best of luck to the anxious kids who are a little too fidgety or the introverted ones who have trouble with eye contact!)

- Observation of verbal cues that could indicate lying, such as contradictions, diversion, or over-explaining

- Direct blaming, citing evidence of guilt (even if that evidence is fabricated—remember, the police *are* allowed to lie to you!)

- Proffering a psychological justification for the crime in order to show sympathy and give a false sense of security to the suspect

- Presenting two questions for the version of events, one of which is more socially redeemable but *both* indicating guilt (in other words, guilt is assumed, and the student isn't given an option!)

- Inferring that displays of strong emotion such as crying indicate guilt

This is some pretty heavy stuff. Law enforcement goes through countless hours of training to learn how to take statements, but school administrators get three hours of education, and they think they are ready to use these tactics responsibly? I don't think so. Also, consider that the Reid Method has come under substantial scrutiny for its role in eliciting false confessions, *particularly* among juveniles. In fact, in 2017, Wicklander-Zulawski & Associates, one of the foremost training services for interrogation techniques for federal and law enforcement agencies, announced in a press release the discontinuation of using the Reid Method after 30 years because of this controversy.[40]

So, even though the student might not be talking to a police officer and might not have a right to the Miranda warning, that does not stop schools from using police techniques on students. A quick story to demonstrate how this can get out of control:

A client called me to say he had received a call about his high school-aged daughter. He said that a male classmate of his daughter's had been accused of emailing a naked picture of himself from his phone to another student's phone. When questioned by a school administrator, the male student denied that he had sent the picture. He told the administrator that my client's daughter had been in possession of his phone at the time that picture was sent, so she must have been the one to send it.

Now, with a little common sense, it should have been obvious to the administrator that the male classmate said that my client's daughter had sent the picture so he could avoid getting in trouble. But the school administrator then questioned the 15-year-old girl. He didn't use common sense; he used his Reid training. He took her into a room and interrogated her for THREE HOURS, trying to coerce a confession out of her.

He outright blamed her. He lied and claimed that other students had corroborated the male classmate's story. He tried to solicit a confession by saying that the punishment would be less severe if she did confess. The girl asked to call her parents, but the administrator would not allow it (even though the school's Code of Conduct stated that if a student asks to call a parent during questioning, the student must be allowed to do so).

My client reported that the girl was in hysterics but maintained her innocence through her tears. Finally, after she begged, the administrator let her call her therapist, who contacted her father, who contacted me. My advice to the dad? "Go to the school, demand they stop questioning her, and take her home." Meanwhile, I dialed the school's attorney to put a stop to this inappropriate process. Fortunately, we were able to rescue the man's daughter, and, after this torture, the school realized the accuser was lying and that he had, in fact, sent the picture.

This is one of the most disgraceful incidents I have ever been involved in. This administrator, with no evidence (other than an allegation from the obviously guilty party), decided he was going to put his training to good use and get the *truth* from my client. Too many hours of watching *Law & Order*, along with his 180 minutes of training in a controversial interrogation method, and he thought he was qualified to use his talents to question my client. He thought he would elicit the truth and be a hero. Instead, all he did was bully and traumatize an obviously innocent child.

At the time this happened, my daughters were 13 and 15. Up to this point, I had told them that if they were ever accused of wrongdoing at school, they should politely tell the school employee that they would like to speak with one of their parents before they answer. But that day, I came home and explained this story to them so they understood the kind of unethical and irresponsible behavior some schools may employ. I wanted to prepare them in case they were ever involved in such a situation. I have always assured them that no matter what anyone threatens them with, it is okay to delay saying anything at all until they can get their thoughts together and speak to a parent or a trusted person.

Most administrators aren't outright jerks and students aren't completely abandoned when it comes to schools and the law. But it's better to be prepared than taken by surprise. Students must understand that they have *absolutely no obligation* to make a statement to any school official. They are free to sit there and refuse to make a statement and any threats the administrator makes should be ignored.

One last note on interrogation in schools: If your kid acknowledges her involvement in wrongful activity, she should focus her statement on her own behavior, not what others are responsible for. Why? If your kid tells on her friends because a school official promises a lighter sentence, rest assured the administrators probably won't follow through on that promise. Not only that, but the temporary relief of blame-sharing won't be worth the long-term damage to their friendships.

DRUGS IN SCHOOL
There are two main issues with drugs in school: 1) possession and 2) selling. While students can get in trouble for possessing or selling all types of illegal drugs, the most prevalent drug is marijuana. Thus, I'll focus my attention on student marijuana possession and selling.

Possession
Thirty years ago, if you wanted to get high during third period, you left the high school grounds with some friends, smoked a joint, and went back to school just in time for fourth period geometry class. But now, with the advent of modern technology, there has been a drastic rise in the prevalence of smoking pot in school buildings. Why? One word: vaping.

For those of you not 'in the know' regarding vape culture, vaporizers are pen-sized devices that heat liquid cannabis and produce a vapor that users inhale, then exhale. This vapor has virtually no smell. This means that kids can smoke discreetly in school parking lots, bathrooms, and hallways without tipping off the teachers. When she was in high school, my youngest daughter told me about a teen who would smoke *in the classroom* and blow the vapor into his sleeve when the teacher's back was turned! I couldn't believe how easy it was.

But just because kids *can* be more discreet about smoking dope doesn't mean they don't get caught. Vape pens fall out of pockets, vape detectors are installed in bathrooms, etc. While it's true that most schools aren't running massive schoolwide drug sweeps without reasonable suspicion, it's critical to educate your teens on the hazards of getting caught with drugs.

Selling
Both of my daughters knew which students at their high school sold drugs. They knew that if they wanted drugs, they could get them (thankfully, my wife and I taught our daughters to be smart enough never to buy drugs at school). The point is that selling drugs in school is *common* and most students know which classmates they could approach to score a bag of weed. But selling drugs in a school is exceedingly risky. If a dealer gets on the wrong side of the wrong person who rats him out to school officials, he'll be facing criminal charges.

Overall, when it comes to pot in school, my advice to students is: *Don't do it. Ever.* It's one thing to get high by your parents' pool with your friends, and it's an entirely different thing to risk having to talk about your drug suspension on your college application, all because you were vaping in the bathroom when a security guard walked in.

Parents: In general, when it comes to the law and school premises, impress upon your teens the importance of staying away from any and all illegal activities on campus. Getting in trouble with police is one thing; getting in trouble with the school administration is a whole other thing that can lead to a whole other host of problems. At minimum, teach your kids to be smart and keep it out of the classroom.

CHAPTER 11

Social media and cell phones

The use of social media and cell phones can have a profound impact on our teens' social lives and mental health. Parents often aren't privy to the depths of their teens' social media and texting activity, and teens often aren't aware that their digital actions can affect them offline as well. This is a comparatively new phenomenon in our society, and parents are still trying to figure out the best way to teach their kids how to be aware that *anything* they do digitally could be open to the world to see. Any mistake teens make online can be exposed at any time (even if it's in a private text!). And both their school and the legal system can hold them accountable for those mistakes.

In this chapter, we'll talk about the social, academic, and legal ramifications of digital world mishaps, and I'll offer advice that you can give your kids to help keep them out of trouble.

SOCIAL RAMIFICATIONS

I am a big believer in allowing children to make mistakes so that they learn from them. The problem is that we now live in a society with the ability to memorialize every little mistake anyone makes, and punishment for those mistakes can rear its ugly head at any time. A thoughtless comment, a retweeted meme, an offensive picture, an angry exclamation—all now can be permanently saved and distributed on the world wide web. Again, this doesn't apply only to public posts on social media. This goes for texting and direct messaging as well.

Picture this:

You're a girl in sixth grade and you text your best friend everything, including your thoughts on all the people you go to school with (some of which aren't so nice because, hey, you're 12). Three years later, in ninth grade, your former best friend is now best friends with one of the girls you said horrible things about, and she shows her the texts. This girl publicly confronts you in the cafeteria about your documented sixth-grade insults, and now you have to deal not only with her but with half the ninth-grade class that overheard your loud argument in the lunchroom and now sees you as an outcast.

It's not fair, but it's the reality we live in. When my oldest daughter was in 10th grade, she got into an argument with the partner she was working with in class. It was a relaxed, shop kind of environment, but my daughter and her partner were both inappropriately loud. If the argument had continued, the teacher probably would have gotten involved and there might have been trouble. Now, if this was all that had happened, I would have had no problem. If one of my children acts inappropriately in school, she must deal with the consequences. But that's not what happened.

What actually happened is that the argument stopped. And why did it stop, you ask? It didn't stop because the teacher got involved or because her schoolmates tried to defuse the situation. It stopped because her classmates took their phones out and started to record it. My daughter, thankfully, stopped the argument as soon as the cameras came out.

When my daughter told me this story, I was astonished. That was her classmates' first instinct? Whatever happened to minding your own business? If my kid hadn't had the wherewithal to stop, she could have become part of a viral video!

I believe everyone is entitled to have a bad day. I believe children should understand when they have done something wrong and try to learn from it, so that they behave better next time. But they shouldn't be permanently shamed because their bad day was recorded, and some kid made it public for all the school (and the world) to see. Unfortunately, this is the world we now live in, so teach your kids to be smart and aware when they are anywhere public.

SCHOOL AND LEGAL RAMIFICATIONS

At what point do the schools get involved? Usually, schools will get involved when there are incidents of bullying, threats, or sexting. If caught, each of these offenses can land your kid in serious trouble not only with the school but in some cases with the law.

Bullying

Where I practice in Long Island, a school has the authority to regulate a bullying incident when it falls under the following definition, drawn from New York State Law:

> *"'Harassment' or 'Bullying' shall mean the creation of a hostile environment by conduct or by threats, intimidation or abuse, including cyberbullying, that*
>
> *a. has or would have the effect of unreasonably and substantially interfering with a student's educational performance, opportunities or benefits, or mental, emotional and/or physical well-being; or*
>
> *b. reasonably causes or would reasonably be expected to cause a student to fear for his or her physical safety; or*
>
> *c. reasonably causes or would reasonably be expected to cause physical injury or emotional harm to a student; or*
>
> *d. occurs off school property and creates or would foreseeably create a risk of substantial disruption within the school environment, where*

it is foreseeable that the conduct, threats, intimidation or abuse might reach school property. Acts of harassment and bullying shall include, but not be limited to, those acts based on a person's actual or perceived race, color, weight, national original, ethnic group, religion, religious practice, disability, sexual orientation, gender or sex. For the purposes of this definition the term 'threats, intimidation or abuse' shall include verbal and non-verbal actions."[41]

As you can see, this definition encompasses a wide variety of behavior both on and off campus. When schools use an all-encompassing standard like "reach school property," they are essentially taking jurisdiction over any communication between two students, wherever they may be. So, even if a kid cyberbullies their classmate from the comfort of his own home, he could still be subject to disciplinary action by the school.

I once represented a high school student who had a private text group with four of his classmates. The students started chatting about another schoolmate and made some disrespectful statements about him. While these comments were unkind, most of the texters believed the subject of their ridicule would never see their comments. Nor did they want him to see the texts. They didn't want to hurt him. The comments weren't said to harass the kid; it was just stupid teenage boys being stupid teenage boys.

The students *believed* that this text group was a private communication among the five of them. They never even considered there could be any ramifications as a result of the things they said. But one of the kids in the chat group showed the texts to the boy they were mocking. The boy took screenshots of the chat, emailed them to the school, and the school filed a Code of Conduct violation against my client and the other boys in the group.

In trying to fight the case, I made the analogy that this kind of conversation is similar to when I was in high school. As kids, we'd kick back and have the same kind of chat in a friend's basement. The difference is that now everything the immature teenage brain thinks of is immortalized for all to see on our electronic devices. To me, it isn't fair to hold kids responsible for statements not intended to harass, especially when they are unaware that their conversations are not, in fact, private.

Unfortunately, this school and most schools I come into contact with do not give much weight to this argument. They feel that teens must understand how to properly conduct themselves on social media and will hold them responsible if they do not.[42] And, regrettably, their misconduct is all too easy to prove. No eyewitness account is needed because the evidence is right there in their chat history.

The lesson here is that while intentional bullying and harassment certainly do happen and the school should hold the student perpetrators responsible for their actions in those cases, there are incidents when schools charge students with harassment because their private conversation was made public as a result of technology. This is why teens should always be careful what they type into their phones, even when they believe they are having a "harmless" private conversation. The school will not care what your intention was; they will only consider the damage done.

Threats

When language, imagery, or actions are used to threaten a student, teacher, academic administrator, or the school in any way, the school can charge the offender with a violation of the Code of Conduct. Not only that: if the threat is a violation of criminal law, then there is a high likelihood that the school will involve the police.

Say, for example, a 14-year-old teenager messages her former best friend, who is now dating her former boyfriend, on Facebook. She types: "I want to kill you." Taken out of context, this could be seen as a serious threat on someone's life. In reality, this is simply the expression of an angry teenage girl who is lashing out and not aware that her words could be used against her. She could face suspension and even legal charges.

Threats can encompass anything from intimidating another student with a promise of violence to taking pictures with weapons and posting them on social media. Unfortunately, as a result of the escalation in school shootings in the last couple of decades, schools must be vigilant in protecting students from perceived threats to their safety. They must treat *any* threat to the student body or the actual school with seriousness. But sometimes, in the school's vigor to be thorough, students get caught up in the disciplinary procedure of both the school and the law for what is, in reality, a simple misunderstanding.

I had a case recently where a kid posted on social media, "Friday is going to be the worst day for everyone." His sister found out about the post 20 minutes later and told him to take it down, since it could be misinterpreted. He immediately took it down and posted a follow-up that said, "I did not want to scare anyone. Friday is my birthday, and I don't have many friends, so it will be a bad day for everyone." Although he quickly corrected himself, at that point, news about his post had already gotten out.

Four hours after the original post, I was watching in real time as parents on the school district's Facebook group were posting things like, "I heard there was a bomb threat," and "I was told that someone said they were going to blow up the high school on Friday." They all swore they were not sending their kids to school the next day and they were going to take action to get to the bottom of it. Because of this hysteria, school officials were forced to act and to suspend this kid for a post that, truthfully, was a plea for help. But instead of receiving help, he became an overnight pariah.

So, what are the consequences of a threat? Depending on the content of the social media post or text, and whether it is viewed as bullying or a direct "threat," students might be suspended from school for just a few days or up to an entire year. If the case is serious enough to go to court, the student will be charged with aggravated harassment or making terroristic threats in juvenile court if under 18 and in criminal court if over 18.

Sexting

Sending illicit photos via social media and via text is common, but it's important that you communicate to your kids that it can have serious legal ramifications. Not only could they find themselves suspended from school for up to a year, but it can be seen in a court of law as "underage pornography".

While the law is created to protect teens, if underage individuals send nude pictures of themselves or classmates, the court can charge them with possession and dissemination of pornography to a minor, which is a *felony*. In a New York case, a 16-year-old boy asked a 15-year-old girl to send him a nude picture. When she did, he shared it with his friends. This is a class D felony, which could have earned him seven years in prison and sex offender registration. Although he did spend time in jail, his sentence was ultimately reduced to a misdemeanor.[42] But he *did* spend time in jail, all for what I'm sure he thought of as a relatively innocent exchange.

Luckily, due to initiatives such as New York's Diversion Program, which allows teens involved in sexting to avoid criminal prosecution by undergoing an educational course, most of these cases will not result in a criminal conviction. However, even with these measures in place, it is still important to impress upon your kids the potential consequences of this charge. From criminal charges to suspension to the embarrassment of having a nude picture that could be shared for all the world to see—if they get caught, they will have to face the music.

The lesson here: Tell your kids not, *under any circumstances*, to take or share nude photos.

WHAT I TELL MY DAUGHTERS

You have to be the one to teach your kids about responsible use of social media. No one else is going to teach them that just one stray comment on Snapchat could lead to lifetime consequences. That said, kids will say things that aren't smart, so it's important for you to model good behavior and monitor their online activity to ensure they are being responsible. Have rules set up for social media use and offer real ramifications for breaking those rules.

Here are the three big lessons I tell my kids when it comes to social media:

1. **Online is forever.** Make it a practice to take a few deep breaths before you hit the "send" button. Whether it's in a public post or a private DM, it has the potential to get out to your classmates, your school, and the world at large. Even just a small one-line post, picture, or ten-second clip could land you in hot water with your school (and in some cases, the law!). Even if you take the post down after five minutes. Even if it's off school premises. If the school can find a link, any link, between the post and the school, you could face exclusion from programs, suspension, and the need to explain your behavior on a college application. Moreover, if it's public, it could impact your relationships and emotional well-being.

   Think of it like this: If you were famous and everyone in the world could see your text or tweet, what would they say? Someday, your post could go viral. I once had a teenage client who had a video of him posted online in which he refused to take off his offensive T-shirt in an airport. The video went viral, and now it is several years later, and he *still* has trouble getting a job, because that video is the first thing that comes up when potential employers search his name.

2. **Even if you think you are being safe, you can still get in trouble.** There is no such thing as being completely private online. I tell my daughters even if you are talking to your best friends, what you say can come back to haunt you. Friendships are fickle and, in most of the cases I see, bullying and harassment actually come from *inside* social circles. In high school, someone could be your best friend one day and turn your post in to the principal the next.

This also goes for being "clever" with fake profiles. Many kids create fake accounts on other social media platforms. (On Instagram, fake accounts are cleverly called "finstas," a combination of "fake" and "Instagram"); kids believe a fake account gives them license to act however they want. Here's the hard truth: it's easy to find out who is behind a social media account. So if you are communicating in a way that would constitute a criminal offense or violation of the school's disciplinary code, it is likely that an investigation would be able to trace these communications back to you.

3. **If you even think, "Should I really post this?" or "Should I really send this?"** *don't.* I'm all about making mistakes as a kid (I made a good share myself), but when it comes to making them online, there is no room for error. If you question whether you should post something or not, there's a reason why. When it comes to social media and technology, one misstep could change your entire life in an instant. Teach your kids to keep their offensive comments, pictures, and videos off their devices. Or, better yet, teach them to abide by the old principle that if they don't have something nice to say, don't say anything at all.

CHAPTER 12

High school disciplinary process

No parent wants to receive a call from the principal saying that their kid is in serious trouble, but it can happen to the best of us. In this chapter, I'll walk you through the high school disciplinary process, from accusation of the offense to the hearing process to the potential consequences of your kid's actions. I'll also give you a few hard-won pieces of advice on how to navigate these sometimes-tricky situations with the school.

ACCUSATION AND NOTIFICATION OF A VIOLATION OF THE SCHOOL CODE OF CONDUCT

What happens after a school accuses a student of violating its Code of Conduct?

First, the school notifies both the student and the parents. In extreme cases in which a crime was committed, such as when weapons, threats, or selling drugs is involved, the school may also notify local law enforcement. Usually, parents will be notified via a phone call as well as a letter mailed or emailed on the same day that the call is made. If a student is removed from school premises as a result of the violation, the school gives the student a letter to take home, which details the following:

- A statement that the school is choosing to remove the student

- A description of the charges against the student

- Parents' right to request an immediate meeting to discuss the charge

Now, barring any immediate danger to persons on campus or an ongoing threat to the academic process, the school will likely bring the student and parents in for an informal meeting before removing him from school premises. If, in the course of this meeting, the parents and child convince school administrators that the charges are not supported by substantial evidence, removal may be overruled.

MEETING WITH THE SCHOOL

In the informal meeting, school officials will lay out the charges against the student. If the student denies the charges in the meeting, administrators must explain to the student why he is being removed and give the student and parents an opportunity to defend the student's version of events. In my experience, this meeting is akin to a mini hearing. The onus is on the parents and the accused student to try to convince school administrators that the child is not guilty of the accusation levied against him.

In the course of this meeting, in my experience, there are the two major possible pitfalls:

1. The kid makes a statement that hurts rather than helps the case.

2. The parent makes a statement that hurts rather than helps the case.

At this point in the disciplinary process, it's rare that a lawyer like me will have been called in to assist. It's unfortunate because this is a time when the student and the parents have an opportunity to make their case. It is also unfortunate because I have seen many incidents in which students or their parents slip into one of the pitfalls I just described.

Since most teens and their parents *won't* have a lawyer like me around in the beginning, if you have the option to talk with your child before he gives a statement, I recommend emphasizing to him that he has the right not to make a statement during this informal meeting. This goes for you as the parent as well. Keep in mind, as I've reiterated on several occasions, in proffering unnecessary information or opinions in this situation, you may unwittingly make things worse for your child.

Both you and your teen should simply answer the questions you are asked. Be respectful but be firm. You have the power to say, "I am here to listen to what you have to say, and I will discuss it with my teen at home and follow up the next day with a statement." You are under no obligation to make a statement by the time you leave the office.

After you meet with the school officials, they will deliberate on the incident and your arguments and decide on the appropriate punishment. This punishment is generally focused on rehabilitation and considers the student's age and maturity, prior record, and character. Punishment can range from simple detention to exclusion from extracurricular clubs and events to suspension.

Some of these remedies/punishments include:

• Supportive intervention

• Behavioral assessment

• Behavioral management plans

• Student counseling

• Corrective classes

• Oral warnings

- Written warnings

- Detention

- Suspension from transportation

- Removal from athletic participation or other school activities

- In-school suspension

- Suspension from school for up to five days

Typically, suspension for minor infractions is five days or less. If your teen has committed a major offense and school officials determine that he should be suspended for more than five days, then the student must go through a superintendent hearing. Unfortunately, in this situation, the outcome is not made completely clear for many students and parents. This is what often happens instead: The parents and student have the initial meeting with the school administrator and the determination is a five-day suspension. They are told that if there is to be a longer suspension, they will get a letter from the superintendent's office. What they don't tell the student and the parents is that almost everyone gets a letter. The administrator lets the family walk out of the office thinking that it may be only a five-day suspension, when he knows full well that the determination of a five-day suspension will always result in the student getting a letter a few days later. That letter instructs the student to be present at a superintendent's hearing, where the full punishment will be considered.

SUPERINTENDENT HEARINGS

If your child gets a notice that the school wants to suspend him for more than five days, he is entitled to what is called a superintendent's hearing. This hearing allows the student a chance to further refute the charges against him. An impartial hearing officer—who is either a superintendent or someone the superintendent designates, such as a staff member or an arbitrator— usually presides over the superintendent's hearing. Either an administrator or the school district's lawyer then represents the district.

The school district then provides evidence for the hearing officer in an attempt to prove the student responsible. The school's burden is to show the student committed the offense by a *preponderance of the evidence*. This means that the school prosecutors need to convince the hearing officer that the student is guilty with more than 50 percent certainty (for comparison, in the criminal courts, the *beyond a reasonable doubt* standard requires a much greater certainty to convict someone).

Believe me, this is a tragically easy standard to meet.

The process is further complicated by the fact that, as we learned in Chapter 10, the school doesn't have to abide by the same due process rules in gathering evidence that they would be restricted to in court. Pretty much any "evidence" can be brought into the hearing, including hearsay. In fact, many times the actual witnesses do not testify; their statements are read into the record by whoever is representing the school. This means it isn't possible to cross-examine the "witnesses," and a simple statement could be taken as "proof." Unfortunately, as a result of the low standard of proof needed and the potentially faulty testimonies allowed as evidence, in my experience, these cases are extremely hard to win. Even if you have a lawyer like me on your side, we are facing a prosecutor and judge who are basically on the same side, and it can be challenging to get them to listen to reason.

What I often do when I get involved in a case like this is try to negotiate a reasonable resolution. Now, if the student tells me he is innocent, and we have reasonable evidence to show this, then we will go to the hearing. However, if I think there is a fair chance the school will find the student responsible, I will see if we can come to an agreement with the school *before* the case goes to a superintendent's hearing.

When determining punishment there are three main issues that the school and the student should be concerned about:

1. What period of time will the student be kept out of school?

2. Will the suspension be on the student's permanent record?

3. Will the student be restricted from certain school activities: sports teams, proms, school clubs, tournaments, etc.?

My goal for any teen client in this situation is to keep the student out of school for the least amount of time with the least restrictions on extracurricular activities. I will also try to reach an agreement with the school: If the student pleads "no contest," then the school consents to expunge the charge from the student's permanent record after a predetermined amount of time, as long as the student stays out of trouble.

MANIFESTATION DETERMINATION HEARINGS

If your child has a learning, behavioral, physical, or emotional disability and has committed an act that violates the school's Code of Conduct, then administrators will hold a manifestation determination hearing. This meeting will determine whether your child's inappropriate behavior is a manifestation of her disability. If your child has a disability, she cannot be punished in the same way as her peers. Usually, if this happens, the school will do a behavior assessment and other evaluations to determine the necessary interventions to help the student.

Be aware, however, that if your child hasn't been officially classified as having a disability, there is little chance they will hold this kind of meeting. If you suspect that your child is struggling with a disability, I cannot stress enough the importance of notifying the school and asking for your child to be evaluated. I will go into more detail on helping kids with disabilities navigate the school system in Chapter 19.

ADVICE FOR PARENTS

If you're a parent facing this situation, I don't envy you or your child. It is often frustrating and can unfortunately be unfair. Let me offer a few pieces of advice:

1. **The school is looking out for the school first. You should look out for your kid first.** Many parents make the mistake of thinking that because administrators are generally kind, good-hearted people, they will be authentic with you and place the interests of your child first. Know that the school has an obligation to uphold the rules that are set out by the school district and to look out for the school's best interests *first*. In other words, school officials might not take you aside and say, "Listen, your kid is in real trouble, and here's exactly what you need to do so she gets in the least amount of trouble." The "right thing" doesn't always happen. That's why it can be helpful to consult professionals like me in these matters. Further, I encourage you to do your own research on school policy and be on the lookout for any indicators that your kid might need special attention for behavioral or learning issues that might have led to her offensive actions.

2. **Don't worry; suspension does not mean your child's education stops.** If a student is suspended, the school is still obligated to educate the student. This usually happens either through private tutors at a local library or a separate afternoon/evening program for all suspended students in that district. This rule extends only to core classes like English and science classes, so unfortunately any additional classes will not be included. The school will make arrangements for any fundamental standardized testing, such as the SAT, that might take place during the suspension.

3. **Private schools work a little differently.** Private schools do not have to adhere to certain state-run school policies and, more

importantly, they are financially motivated. It is for that reason that I rarely get clients from private schools. I find that private schools are all over the place in their policies and procedures. Many of these schools do not want to do anything to students that might affect the next tuition payment; nevertheless, many schools will summarily dismiss a student for bad behavior. I was recently consulted by a parent who had teenagers in two different private schools; the kids were accused of the same unacceptable social media behavior. One student was expelled. The other was given a warning and told not to do it again.

4. **During a hearing, do not say anything unless it will directly help your child.** The goal during a hearing is to convince the hearing officer that there is not enough evidence to find the student guilty. Because the parent is usually at the hearing, and they may be given an opportunity to speak, I discuss with them in advance what they will say, and then I tell them to stick to that statement. I want everything they say to be directly relevant to the allegations and helpful to their child. The hearing is *not* a time to bring up old gripes or try to "make a point."

Here's an example of how saying the wrong thing can end badly:

One of the very first high school students I represented had been accused of breaking into his school with three friends during the summer break and stealing vending machine supplies and laptops and inciting general mayhem. The kids were undeniably guilty. They had been recorded on the school's camera and also admitted to it. But the school door had been left open, so the kids didn't technically "break in." But they did steal the supplies and cause damage to school property.

During the hearing with school officials, my client's father asked me if he could make a statement on his son's behalf. He told me he simply wanted to say what a good kid his son was. What he actually did was this: he looked the superintendent right in the eye and said, **"Mr. So-and-So, wouldn't you agree that if somebody leaves their** *convertible car open with their keys in it, then another person gets into that car and drives away, isn't the person who was stupid enough to leave their keys in the engine somewhat responsible?"*

As you can imagine, he did *not* make the case for his kid. My aim was to make his kid look remorseful for his actions, not put blame on the school! Believe me, school officials did not respond well to that. I still remember the look on the superintendent's face as my client's dad was making this statement. His face got red, his eyes bulged out of his head, and he proceeded to tell my client and his parents that even though it cost the district more money to educate the student off school grounds, he was happy to spend the money so this student wouldn't be a thorn in his side for the next year. To this day, if a parent wants to speak on behalf of their kid, I tell them that they need to tell me *exactly* what they're going to say and *stick to it* in the hearing.

5. **Appeals are generally useless.** In my experience, if you take the case to the District or State Board of Education, or even to the courts, they will typically side with the schools. So, it is not usually a realistic option to assume that if the hearing doesn't go well, you can win in an appeal.

6. **The disciplinary process in elementary and middle school is generally the same, with one difference.** Most of what I have shared goes for elementary and middle school as well. The key distinction is that any disciplinary issues before ninth grade do not need to be disclosed on a college application, which is the primary concern for most high school students.

As I said at the outset, no parent or teen wants to be put in this situation *ever*. But if this does happen to you, these guidelines can help you navigate the sometimes-treacherous waters of the high school disciplinary process.

CHAPTER 13

Greek life and hazing

On many campuses, college culture is synonymous with 'Greek life.' Each year, freshmen attend rush events anxiously hoping one of the sororities or fraternities accepts them. There are several benefits to joining the Greek culture, such as a sense of camaraderie, lifelong bonds with your brothers or sisters, invitations to exclusive parties, danceathons, post-college job opportunities, and philanthropic work.

It's no wonder that many students who are living away from home for the first time gravitate toward this lifestyle. Everyone wants to belong, and this is a fast, easy way to acquire a group of friends. As a parent, however, it's important to be aware of the risks that come with involvement in these organizations. More specifically, it's important to know the dangers of hazing.

Now, if you've never been a part of a fraternity or sorority, allow me to speak from personal experience. I never planned on joining a fraternity, but three weeks into my freshman year, a fraternity gave me a bid and I became a pledge. Most of the activities were innocent, but some ... well, let's just say that in retrospect we could have been a bit safer and a bit smarter. Thankfully, no one in my fraternity was seriously injured, but it would have taken just one wrong move for something terrible to happen.

In this chapter, we'll explore what hazing is, the dangers of hazing, the potential consequences of hazing, and how to talk to your kids about hazing on college campuses.

A BRIEF BREAKDOWN OF HAZING

For those of you unfamiliar with Greek life on college campuses, hazing is a way of inducting a new member into a group. Typically, existing members put the inductees through a series of strenuous, often humiliating, tasks designed to train and challenge them. It's an odd tradition whereby college kids have an inordinate amount of power and influence over their only-slightly-younger peers.

While hazing is most often associated with fraternities and sororities, it's not confined to Greek culture. Hazing is a prevalent part of the culture in many other collegiate organizations, such as athletic teams, club sports, and performing arts troupes. You may be surprised to learn that between 50 and 75 percent of these groups participate in hazing![43] Look at the breakdown in the chart of hazing in college organizations:

Percent of students in each activity that experienced at least one hazing behaviour[44]

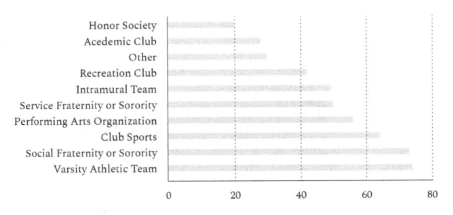

Whatever the organization, hazing can be as innocuous as learning to recite the Greek alphabet, memorizing the organization's history, interviewing current members, or volunteering at the local nursing home. However, hazing also often involves binge drinking, humiliation, physical activity to the point of exhaustion, and other dangerous activities that put your teen at risk. Yet while a college organization may try to convince their pledges that they are playing it safe, your teen should know that there is real danger involved. A 19-year-old or 20-year-old often does not have the sense of responsibility and fortitude needed to ensure the safety of their 18-year-old peers.

For example:

In February 2017, college sophomore Timothy Piazza made major headlines when he died from falling down a flight of stairs and suffering serious internal injuries after his fraternity brothers forced him to drink lethal amounts of alcohol during hazing at a party. The brothers waited a full 12 hours before calling 911. By the time Timothy went in for surgery, it was too late.[45]

I remember in my junior year, a pledge from another fraternity died when he and his pledge brothers were told to go into a lake on campus. There was a live wire in the lake. When he got close to it, he was electrocuted and killed. While none of the brothers intended serious harm to the student, it was a horrifying accident that I have never forgotten.

Even if most hazing doesn't lead to these extreme consequences, it can have serious physical, psychological, and educational impacts on students. While it may seem like the norm, that does not mean it should be taken lightly.

SCHOOL POLICY

In colleges, hazing is strictly banned. But there is little way to enforce anti-hazing policies without monitoring students 24/7. The school will usually take action against organizations only if a specific complaint is made to the Office of Student Conduct or if they are notified of the involvement of law enforcement or emergency services.

In lieu of constant surveillance, most schools try to be proactive by setting up rules for Greek initiations that are designed to educate and protect. These include:

- GPA minimums

- A designated and finite period for the "new member" process

- A required hazing education course

- Code of Conduct guidelines that prohibit specific hazing activities

- A ban on drinking alcohol when pledges are present

Obviously, having a high GPA and watching a few videos does not prevent a kid from binge drinking or encouraging other kids to binge drink. So, these policies can sometimes be ineffective.

GETTING INTO TROUBLE

Not only can hazing lead to physical or emotional danger but, if a school becomes aware of illicit activities, they can bring charges against the organization. If a complaint is made and an investigation is under way, there are two concerns for the involved Greek life students:

1. Will the organization suffer any penalties?

2. Will I personally get into trouble?

If an organization is found responsible for a violation of the school's Code of Conduct, there are numerous penalties they can incur. For example, let's look at my alma mater, the State University of New York at Albany, which has struggled to keep its Greek life under control. Out of 21 fraternities in 2019, two were de-recognized, two had their charters revoked, five were currently suspended, four were on probation, and one had a *cease and desist* order filed against it. In all, only one third of the 21 fraternities were actually in good standing with the school.

Fraternity or sorority students in penalized Greek life organizations should be concerned if the offenses committed were particularly egregious or if their own guilt is obvious. In those cases, there may be an individual disciplinary proceeding for accused students, which could result in punishments ranging from warning to expulsion.

WHAT HAPPENS WHEN THE GROUP IS NO LONGER RECOGNIZED?

When Greek organizations lose their status of being recognized organizations on campus, it puts members into a difficult situation. When an organization is de-recognized, suspended, or not allowed on campus, former members are subject to a whole host of violations that require little proof for the school to act on. Violations include actions such as running a rush event (where new members are recruited), inducting a new pledge class (where new members are 'educated' or formally join the organization), and/or having a party sponsored by the group. If students are caught, they could face suspension and potential expulsion.

I once represented a student whose fraternity had been de-recognized. His school was investigating whether the fraternity activities were ongoing, and they found an online picture of eight kids, two of whom were wearing the disbanded fraternity's T-shirt, including my client. This photo was taken 2,000 miles away from campus, but the school used it to help make their case that the fraternity was still in existence and attempted to punish the involved members.

WHAT TO TELL YOUR KIDS

It's difficult to say "no" if your kid wants to join a fraternity or sorority, even knowing the risks. There are, as I said, enormous social benefits to joining these organizations. Some of my closest friends to this day are from my fraternity. That's why it's important to have a talk with your kid about the potential consequences of pledging before you send them off to school on their own. That way, they have tools to be smart about the risks they take. It takes only one mistake for them to get suspended, expelled, or even seriously injured.

WHAT I'D TELL MY DAUGHTERS

Neither of my daughters expressed interest in joining a sorority, but if they did, here's what I'd tell them:

1. **Always be upfront about your concerns, even if you feel silly.** Find someone who seems "real" in the organization and ask her the straightforward questions: "I know you said we don't need to drink, but is that really the case? Just so you know, I don't drink and don't intend to."

2. **Take responsibility for yourself.** Don't take organization members at their word if they say that they're "responsible." Brothers and sisters might try to convince you that the horror stories you've heard are overhyped. However, even though they are older than you, they are still young. They might not be capable of taking care of you when you are in a vulnerable position.

3. **Know your limits.** Part of taking responsibility for yourself means being aware of your limits. Bad things can happen when you drink too much. Don't allow members to goad you into drinking beyond your limit. It could lead to serious health complications. Stand up for yourself like this: "Listen, I have already taken 4 shots. I can't drink any more. Call me lame or whatever you want, but I just can't do any more." If they keep pushing or you feel like they are violating your physical or psychological health at any time, remember that you always have the option to walk away.

4. **Keep up with your schoolwork.** I was allowed to pledge the first semester of my freshman year. I am pretty sure that between the classes I dropped and my subpar GPA, I might have

single-handedly made the school take a step back and decide that it's not a great idea for first-semester students to pledge. In my sophomore year, they changed the rule so that freshman could only pledge in the spring semester.

5. **Once you are a member, you must be responsible.** Some of the members may attempt to put the pledges in a dangerous situation. You should always be the responsible one in the room. Make sure there is no extreme danger, and that drugs or alcohol are not used during pledge activity.

6. **If the school has specific rules for your Greek organization, you must abide by those rules, even if your organization doesn't.** If the school tells your fraternity that you cannot have a pledge class, and someone complains to the school that they were pledging and you and the other members were hazing them, you could be in serious trouble.

Greek life could be a fulfilling experience for your teen, but it's important to make her aware of the dangers. Teach your teen to be smart. Teach her to be responsible. At the end of the day, she is the only one who can look out for herself.

CHAPTER 14

Drugs and alcohol in college

I've said it before and I'll say it again: There is a high likelihood that after kids hit college, they will drink. There is also a good chance they will try pot or other drugs. And they may engage in either or both of these activities on a *regular basis*. Don't believe me? Here are a few statistics.

THE STATISTICS

According to a 2018 report from the National Institute on Alcohol Abuse and Alcoholism, 54.9 percent of college students aged 18 to 22 drank in the previous month. Almost 37 percent of those students surveyed reported binge drinking.[46] And, according to the Substance Abuse and Mental Health Services Administration (SAMHSA), 1 in 5 college students reported using an illegal drug in the previous month.[47]

While drinking and smoking marijuana are common and often overlooked on college campuses, that does not mean that your teen can't get into trouble. It's important to teach your teen how to be responsible while away at school. In this chapter, we'll look at school policy on drugs and alcohol, the consequences and risks of getting caught, and the advice you can pass on to your teen, so his future won't be impacted by a few not-so-smart decisions.

SCHOOL POLICY

The *official* collegiate policy in the U.S. is that anyone under the age of 21 cannot imbibe or possess alcohol, marijuana, or any other illicit drug on campus. Unofficially, however, schools are typically aware that their students experiment with drugs and alcohol and have varying degrees of tolerance for their students' actions, ranging from turning a blind eye to more severe measures like expulsion.

A school's tolerance depends largely on the school's culture. For example, I find that smaller, private schools have less tolerance for drugs and alcohol than big state universities. A violation at a large state university could lead to a warning and a mandatory class, while that same violation at a small private school could lead to a more serious penalty such as removal from campus housing (but that is not always the case).

That said, most schools don't *want* to suspend their students for a one-time violation. Many schools simply want to ensure that their students use cannabis and alcohol responsibly. This is why it is common for schools to implement a Code of Conduct that lays out specific, tiered penalties for drug and alcohol use on campus. It usually works something like this:

Tier 1: First offense with drugs or alcohol results in taking a class, writing an essay on drug or alcohol abuse, incurring a fine, or simply receiving an official warning. Parents may also be notified.

Tier 2: Second offense results in taking another class and possible probation.

Tier 3: Third offense earns a suspension or removal from campus housing.

In my experience, expulsion for drugs or alcohol is rare, but it does happen. Fortunately, I have not encountered any schools that put this kind of violation on a student's transcript.

Most of these cases are kept within the confines of the school. Since it is usually obvious when a student violates school policy, and students are quick to confess when caught in the act, it makes handling the issue "in-house" simple. If a student genuinely believes he did not commit the offense he is accused of, he can go through the disciplinary process and ask for a hearing. I *do not* recommend this course of action if a student is obviously guilty. Going this route will almost certainly lead to conviction and a potentially harsher punishment. Proving drug or alcohol possession is a fairly simple process. Schools may choose to involve police for more serious violations, such as possessing hard drugs like cocaine, heroin, or prescription pills, or selling drugs on school premises. In these situations, the offending student will be arrested and most likely kicked off campus.

HOW STUDENTS GET CAUGHT

Typically, students get caught with drugs or alcohol in one of four scenarios:

- At orientation

- During a room check

- At parties or loud gatherings

- When a student is injured as a result of drugs or alcohol

At Orientation

I can't overstate how often this happens. Kids are away from home for the first time in their lives. They've heard the stories and seen the movies about college that made it look like one continuous party. So, they bring beer, and some weed, and the next thing you know, the dorm is trashed with toilet paper, water is everywhere, and there are a few students with magic marker on their faces passed out in the common area. Before school even starts, these students may be suspended or prohibited from living on campus. I know this might sound extreme—and it is—but these things do happen. And while your child may not even be the one to bring the beers and get blackout drunk, if others cause damage and your kid had a few beers with the gang, he will most likely be looped in with the troublemakers.

During a Room Check

Most colleges' Codes of Conduct and/or Residential Life Housing Agreements state a basic rule for living on campus that goes something like this: Authorized university personnel can enter an on-campus room at any time—either on suspicion of illegal activity or a violation of school policy, for maintenance or repairs, in the event of emergencies, or inspection for inspection's sake.

Anyone who enters a student's room—the RA, the cleaning people, the maintenance people, *whoever*—and sees any signs of drugs or alcohol (or *any* illegal activity for that matter: weapons, fake IDs, etc.) could report the student, and the school could subsequently charge the student. That's why it's important that students not leave items such as ashtrays, joints, bongs, or bottles of alcohol in plain view in their room. Ever. That said, in instances where a school official enters a student's room for maintenance or, say, a simple room check, he is restricted to reporting on only what is in plain view. He can't, for example, rifle through the student's desk drawers or take a peek in the fridge to see if they're stashing a six-pack or a bottle of wine.

Now, if an RA or campus police officer have reasonable grounds to believe a student is committing a crime or violating school policies, the rules are different. They may enter and search your room with almost no search restrictions. If the RA believes there is drinking going on in your room, it would be reasonable and within her rights to search the mini-fridge, look in the back of the closet, and take a whiff of the big red cup a student is holding. If she gets a report that someone was doing bong hits in their dorm room, when she walks in, she may look for that bong in the drawers, under the bed, in the bathtub—anywhere a student might think to hide it. And she probably *will* find it if it's there.

At Parties or Large Gatherings

If a teen holds a party on campus and it gets too loud or too crowded, and the RA decides to stop by and finds everyone with red plastic cups full of jungle juice, not only will the host get caught but so might everyone in the room. Adding insult to injury, because some schools have limitations on the number of people allowed in a room at one time, the school could slap the hosting student with a double violation if there are too many kids in the room.

When a Student Is Injured as a Result of Drugs or Alcohol

If students need to call an ambulance, there is a possibility that both the injured student and the students involved in supplying the drugs or alcohol to the injured party could face drug or alcohol violation charges from the school.

WHAT I TELL MY DAUGHTERS

As you know by now, most college students will drink and smoke pot, so I don't think that telling them not to do it is effective. I do believe, however, that you can teach your kids to be smart about drinking and smoking marijuana. Here's what I tell my college-age daughters:

1. **Be smart.** This is my #1 rule for almost everything in this book. In the case of drugs and alcohol in college, here are a few things you can do to "be smart":

   - Don't leave your vape pen, bong, or beer bottles out in plain view in your dorm room.

- Don't try cramming 27 kids into your two-person dorm room to play a raucous round of Beer Pong.

- Don't smoke pot on the front steps of your dorm building, right underneath your RA's window.

- Don't bring booze to orientation and get kicked out before your first day of college.

Don't be that kid. You're smarter than that.

2) **It might not seem fair but understand that you're taking a risk each time you engage in these activities.** Yes, you may have been drinking in your room for weeks or months or even years before getting caught. Then, one night, you and your friends make a little too much noise and get busted by the RA. It may seem unfair, but just because you didn't get caught all the other times doesn't mean you are exempt from the rules. *Each time* you drink or smoke some pot, you are taking a risk. If caught, be prepared to face the consequences of your actions. Take ownership of your mistakes with grace.

3) **Know the environment.** Be aware of whether the policies for drugs and alcohol on your campus are strict or lenient. I know most students don't actually read the school handbook or pay attention at orientation, but it's easy to ask around to take the temperature of tolerance on your campus. Also, be sure to do some reconnaissance for your dorm building and your RA. Some RAs might let you off with a simple warning ("Hey, guys, put it away.") and some may issue an official write-up.

On my college campus, most students were open about smoking pot and almost never got in trouble, but a buddy of mine had a very strict RA. He was caught smoking pot twice and was thrown off campus permanently. So even if your college is generally lenient, your individual RA might not be.

4) **If you have more than one violation, consider moving off campus.** Say you got caught twice and you plan to keep drinking and smoking pot. My advice is to move off-campus, where you can engage in these activities without violating school policies. It is not worth the risk of getting caught a third time and being suspended or, worse, expelled.

5) **Don't sell. Ever.** Even if you think it's no big deal ("I'm just getting some for my friend"), don't do it. Many states consider a "delivery" or "transfer" of drugs to be a sale. You are setting yourself up to be caught as a dealer, opening the door to the police issuing criminal charges.

6) **Pot and booze are one thing; hard drugs are another.** Keep in mind that while smoking pot and drinking are common activities that schools are used to dealing with, if you are caught with hard drugs, you will likely face more serious consequences. Moreover, as you know, abusing hard drugs and some prescription pills is very dangerous. Don't do hard drugs. Period.

I'll say it once more: there is a high probability that your kid will drink and maybe smoke a little pot in college. The best thing you can do for your college kid is to teach her to be smart about it, if and when she does.

CHAPTER 15

Plagiarism

Plagiarism in academic institutions is surprisingly common. How common? The International Center for Academic Integrity reports that a whopping 60 percent of undergraduates admit to cheating in some form.[48]

WHAT IS PLAGIARISM?

According to *Merriam-Webster Dictionary*[49], "plagiarize" has two definitions:

> to steal and pass off (the ideas or words of another) as one's own: use (another's production) without crediting the source

> to commit literary theft: present as new and original an idea or product derived from an existing source

Any plagiarism that infringes on an author's intellectual property rights can result in federal criminal charges. Anytime a person creates an original work and records it on a tangible medium, such as in an audio recording or on a written document, U.S. law grants the creator ownership of the copyright to their creation. The Fair Use Doctrine of the U.S. Copyright Law[50] permits use of copyrighted works in subsequent works if, and only if, the user credits the original author.

While most college students won't be subject to federal criminal charges for plagiarizing their English Lit 101 paper on George Orwell, they can be subject to a number of penalties from their university. In an academic context, plagiarism includes intentional acts such as:

- Directly copying another's works without citation

- Copying from another person's exam

- Soliciting an outside entity to create or complete an assignment on your behalf

- Resubmitting works from one class for another class (self-plagiarism)

- Improperly citing resources, intentionally and unintentionally

When I was in college, it was easy to plagiarize and not get caught. You could hand in a paper that a friend had used the year before or call up a person listed in the classifieds and hire her for a few bucks to write your paper and mail it to you. Unless your professor had an excellent memory or the ghostwriter wrote the same paper for a number of your classmates, chances are you'd be in the clear.

Today, as a result of the technological revolution, it is easier than ever for students to plagiarize. They have unlimited resources at their fingertips. However, it is also easier than ever to get caught. Teachers have access to plagiarism tracker software like www.turnitin.com and https://copyleaks.com and online school databases of previously submitted papers that make detecting plagiarism as simple as the press of a button.

It's important to talk with your teen about the consequences of plagiarizing, particularly at the college level. Plagiarism that may have simply landed him in an uncomfortable conversation with the teacher in high school could, at the college level, be a mistake that permanently affects his future employment.

PLAGIARISM IN COLLEGE

In my experience, there are two main issues with plagiarism cases at schools:

1. **The definition of plagiarism is vague.** If you need help on a project, at what point does it cross over into plagiarism? For example, imagine a student hires an English tutor. The student asks the tutor to review his latest paper. If the tutor writes half of the paper for the student, that is obviously plagiarism. But what if the tutor merely suggests edits? Is that plagiarism? Even though it may seem innocuous, some schools might say yes.

2. **Schools will still charge you if you unintentionally plagiarize.** Some students know exactly what they're doing when they try to pass off someone else's work as their own. Other students do not mean to plagiarize, but they make an error in citing their resources, or they "essentially" give credit to the author. Even though they might have made an honest mistake, the school can still charge these students with plagiarism. The school doesn't consider the student's *intent* when charging them, only the behavior. Truthfully, it would be harder for the school to prove every offense if they had to prove the student's *intent*. For students, arguing that plagiarism was unintentional may help lessen the penalty, but it will not prevent them from being charged or being found responsible for an offense.

Often, if a student is caught plagiarizing, and a professor or teaching assistant suspects that it was the result of an honest mistake, she will try to work with the student one-on-one to remedy the error without punishment. However, there are always overambitious TAs or hyper-strict professors who refuse to accept naiveté as an excuse, so it is better to learn to be cautious than be caught.

PENALTIES

So, what happens if a student does get accused of plagiarism? Depending on the severity of the conviction, penalties may include:

• Getting a zero on the assignment

• Getting a grade knocked down one letter (e.g., from a B to a C)

• Failing the class

• Probation

• Suspension

• Expulsion

• A permanent mark on the transcript

While most incidents of plagiarism won't appear on a student's permanent college record, keep in mind that some postgraduate programs and professions have a strict admission process. It is likely, for those, that interviewers will ask if the student has ever been found responsible for plagiarism. As tempting as it may be in those cases to lie about his involvement, my advice to the student is this: Don't. It is far too easy through a little simple sleuthing to uncover the truth. To interviewers, it looks better if you show humility and remorse rather than undertake subterfuge.

WHAT TO DO IF YOU ARE ACCUSED OF PLAGIARISM

Typically, if a student calls me and confesses that he has copied half his paper from Chegg.com and is facing a zero on his assignment, I usually tell them that, because it would be pretty hard to win the hearing, the best thing to do is take the zero. A zero is not the end of the world. In cases such as these, where the school will have ample evidence to find the student responsible and the punishment is comparatively mild, I think the sensible action is to accept responsibility and the punishment.

However, while in many college plagiarism cases the guilt is obvious, in some instances the incident is more subjective. If a student knows that she is truly innocent or is facing unreasonable consequences (that is, expulsion for plagiarizing two sentences of a paper), I recommend scheduling a hearing and hiring a lawyer (like me) to help build the case. Then let a panel decide the student's fate.

HEARINGS

In plagiarism cases that go to a hearing, the student should come prepared with as much evidence as possible to prove her innocence. When a student hires me to appeal school decisions, 90 percent of the time the recording I hear of the student's argument in the first hearing sounds something like this: "I swear I didn't cheat. You will ruin my life if you suspend me!" End of argument. There is often no presentation of evidence or concrete, detailed arguments to show why there was no plagiarism. These thin emotional arguments never convince a panel. The student needs facts, evidence, or testimony to actively refute the allegations.

Here is a good example of what students should do in plagiarism hearings:

In one of my cases, the school accused a student of cheating in her upper-level science course. She was innocent, and we needed to show that to the panel. Together, we created an oral argument and a 70-page written document that walked the panel through her process of answering each of the complex assignment questions and explained how she reached these conclusions herself and identified where she made mistakes in the process. The result was that the panel found her not responsible, because we were so detailed in our argument (and, in all honesty, they may not have understood all the high-level scientific information she was explaining to them). The lesson here is that the decision makers will listen to evidence and to arguments.

WHAT I TELL MY DAUGHTERS
From my experience, here is what I tell my daughters about plagiarism:

1. **Even if you think you're being clever, you're not.** I once had a client who submitted a paper he bought online for his class. In order to avoid being caught by the plagiarism trackers, he changed all the important words with the handy help of his thesaurus. The result was a paper that sounded as if it had been written by someone with only a vague concept of the English language. It was ridiculous and, of course, the professor knew right away what he had done.

2. **Technology is not your friend.** Sites like Chegg.com, which purport to be a "homework help" site, offer "tutors" who will essentially write your paper for you. Teachers know this, and believe me, if they run a paper that has been written by Chegg "tutors" through the plagiarism tracker system, you will get caught. Chegg also has a policy of working with college officials when they are investigating allegations of plagiarism or academic misconduct. They will turn over IP addresses and communications with regard to the offense being investigated, making it easier to show that the student plagiarized.

   But technology can mess you up in more ways than one:
   I once had a client who wrote a paper via Google Docs. The teacher logged into her Google Doc and saw that another person had been "shared" on the document. Through a little detective work, the teacher saw that the other person had written the last third of the paper. The teacher used this incident to accuse the girl of plagiarism. The girl claimed she was just logging into her friend's

computer because hers had died, which was quickly and robustly debunked by the academic panel.

3. **College is not high school.** The reality is that cheating is rampant in high schools, primarily because high schools do not use the same resources as a college does to detect cheating. And when students get in trouble, it rarely has any long-term lasting effects. So, they go to college thinking they can copy from their friend in Psych 101 or hand in the identical homework that was done with three other students. What may not have been noticed in high school has a good chance of being noticed in college.

4. **Be careful of working with other students.** Between at-home learning during the pandemic, online testing, and texting, it is easier than ever for students to work together on assignments or tests. But beware: If a teacher catches one student copying from another student, both students could be held responsible and penalized. Even if you think you're just "helping out a friend" by letting him look at your paper, realize that in the eyes of the school you are just as guilty as the friend who cheated using your work. The school can and will charge you with academic misconduct.

5. **Learn to cite properly.** I've seen so many students succumb to penalties because of unintentional, improper citations. Take the time to familiarize yourself with the best way of citing your papers. If you're unsure, check with your professor.

6. **Just don't plagiarize.** I have clients tell me they have plagiarized because they felt they had no choice. They were desperate and down to the wire because they were struggling with the subject matter, or life got in the way, or they simply procrastinated a little too long. School, for many students, can be stressful, and it can feel like missing one assignment can lead to a lifetime of

failure. But here is my advice when a student finds themselves in that situation: Write the bad paper. Get the bad grade. It's not the end of the world. It's better to be a student who didn't get a good grade because he failed to do the work than a student who got suspended because he got caught hiring someone to write the paper for him.

Plagiarism may be common, but that doesn't mean that it's acceptable. Ever. Talk with your college-age students about the importance of doing their own work. It's better to be a B- student with integrity intact than an A+ student facing suspension.

CHAPTER 16

Academic misconduct

Plagiarism is the most prevalent form of academic misconduct, but there are other types of academic misconduct that you and your teen should be aware of. So, let's zoom out and talk about academic misconduct more broadly. We'll start with an example:

> I once represented a student who had hired a "tutor" to log on to his student account with his unique login code and answer complex physics problems on his behalf. The student promised to pay the tutor for two hours of work but, when he was through, paid him for only one. The tutor told my client, "You will regret it if you don't pay what you owe." My client (in a not-so-smart move) still didn't pay him what he'd promised. As he had threatened, the tutor went to the YouTube page where the teacher had posted the problem and made a comment that implicated the student and provided the login codes to prove his wrongdoing. The teacher promptly reported my client to the academic board.

As you can see, this case does include an incident of plagiarism, because the contractor did complete problems on my client's behalf, and it also includes other forms of academic misconduct. The plagiarism was the act itself, but the process of soliciting the plagiarist act in itself was also academic misconduct. Namely, my client paid someone to do work, and he shared sensitive login information with a nonstudent. These offenses are just as serious, if not more so, than the plagiarism itself. My client's punishment was an "F" in the class, but he was allowed to stay at the university. He was lucky.

Here are some other examples of non-plagiarism academic misconduct I've seen throughout my career:

- Lying about the number of hours completed during a school internship

- Submitting fake transcripts to other colleges

- Lying about a family member dying in order to get an extension for an assignment or test

- Breaking into the school computer system to change grades

- Beginning an online test before a proctor is present

- Continuing to work on a timed test after the time is up

- Attempting to bribe TAs or teachers to change a grade

- Claiming fake medical procedures in order to get an extension for an assignment

- A dozen students all working on the same assignment on a shared document

- Students taking a test while sharing answers in a text group

It's important to note that even if a superior is in on a student's act of academic misconduct, the student will be held liable. I had a case where a group of students had to do certain procedures, and their teachers allowed them to fudge the results. Although the students knew what they were doing was wrong, they continued their actions because the superiors allowed it. The superiors had apparently been allowing this kind of academic misconduct for years. When the school found out, they charged the students with academic misconduct violations and fired the faculty responsible. The lesson here is that it's important that students cultivate the awareness and self-possession to identify when their actions are wrong, even in the face of encouragement from their advisors.

GETTING ACCUSED OF ACADEMIC MISCONDUCT

Many times, guilt in academic misconduct is cut and dried. If, for example, a student hires another student to take an in-person test in their place, there's a pretty good chance the professor will notice there's a student present who hasn't been there for the rest of the semester. Or let's say that a student hires someone on another continent to complete an online assignment on his behalf. When the school tracks the IP address, they can assert that there is no way the student managed to make it from Southeast Asia back to her dorm room in the span of six hours. The case is obvious and easy to prove with a little help from technology.

However, as with plagiarism, there are some incidents when guilt is not so clear. In those cases, I encourage students to take their case to a hearing if they believe they have a good chance of winning. For example, if four students work together on three group assignments and take a test on those assignments, they will most likely have similar answers. If they are then accused of plagiarism, it could be unclear whether they illicitly collaborated or whether they simply had similar answers because they worked together.

Generally, the potential penalties for academic misconduct are the same as for plagiarism. However, be aware that for serious violations, there can be serious consequences. I get a lot of inquiries to represent students in academic misconduct cases, but I only take the case in three situations:

1. Suspension or expulsion is on the line.

2. Their future career is on the line.

3. They are genuinely innocent.

If a student is caught in the act of academic misconduct and the punishment is that a grade is reduced or they're given an "F" for the class, it often doesn't make sense for me to represent her. If that's the worst consequence a student is facing, my help probably won't get her a lighter punishment.

If, however, a student is facing a more serious consequence, such as suspension or expulsion, or if they are genuinely innocent, it is usually worth the fight. Being found responsible for this kind of violation could significantly limit a student's post-graduate opportunities. It could hinder her applications for advanced-degree programs such as medical school or law school, or employment applications to work in industries such as finance or government, where she will be asked if she has ever been accused or convicted of academic misconduct.

In the end, my advice on academic conduct is the same as on plagiarism: Tell your kids not to do it. Ever. The temporary gain is never worth the price they could pay.

CHAPTER 17

Title IX and sex offenses

Title IX of the Education Amendments Act of 1972 is the law that prevents sex-based discrimination directed at students or faculty in any colleges or universities that accept federal funding.[51] Acts of discrimination include exclusion based on gender, sexual harassment, sexual assault, rape, sexual battery, and sexual coercion.

In this chapter, I'll talk about Title IX in action, policy changes that you and your teen should know, and how to talk to your teen about Title IX.

Please note: This chapter, like the rest of the chapters in this book, focuses on the circumstances that arise when a student is accused of a bad act. As a defense attorney, I represent a range of clients, including those who are accused of a wide range of Title IX violations, the great majority of them being allegations of lack of affirmative consent. I recognize that Title IX offenses are a complex and sensitive subject, and I recognize that sex offenses on college campuses do exist. The issue of consent comes up in a lot of these cases, which can be challenging and emotionally laden. Before you continue reading, I want to reassure you that I fully believe that it is *completely unacceptable* for anyone to engage in any sexual interaction without first obtaining affirmative consent from the other party.

THE TITLE IX HISTORY

In 1972, the U.S. government enacted the Title IX policy to help curb widespread sex-based discrimination on federally funded campuses.

While this was effective at implementing greater access and participation for female athletes in college, many people believed it didn't go far enough to curtail incidents of discrimination and sexual misconduct.

Unfortunately, in the process of trying to gain more rights for complainants, schools and the government took away the right to due process for the accused. In 2011, the federal government issued a "Dear Colleague" letter to federally funded schools encouraging a reinterpretation of the existing law.[52] Many schools understood that failure to adhere to the new interpretation could result in a loss of federal funding even though this threat was not specifically stated in the letter. So, they complied with the new guidance, even if it was unfair to the accused. Some of the more controversial proposed modifications included:

- Investigation of sexual harassment or assault allegations, even in the absence of formal complaints

- Investigation of sexual harassment or assault allegations, even if police investigated and determined the complaint was unfounded

- Prohibition of mediation, even if the accuser preferred informal resolution

- Requirement of using a lower standard of "preponderance of evidence" for accusation and conviction rather than "clear and convincing evidence."[53] (This means that the accuser only needs to show that the situation was "more likely than not," which means that even if the arbitrator is only 51 percent sure that the event happened, the accused could be convicted.)

- Discouragement of permitting cross-examination of the accuser. (This makes it challenging to expose any inconsistencies or falsehoods in the accuser's story.)

• Requiring "timely" resolution (usually within 60 days) and limited access to evidence pre-hearing. (This makes it challenging for the accused to have adequate resources and time to develop a substantial defense.)

In 2017, after a backlash from students and institutions, the Department of Education withdrew the proposed guidance of the "Dear Colleague" letter.[54] Then, in 2020, a new law went into effect. It reinstated the need for a formal complaint, allowed cross-examination of the accuser; permitted more access and time to review evidence presented by both the accused and the accuser; and disallowed a single entity from acting as an investigator, a prosecutor, and the judge. The statement also clarified that schools were not at risk of losing federal funding for using their own discretion in providing the accused with the right to a fair hearing.[55]

The future of Title IX policy is precarious. During the writing of this book, the new federal administration announced they would seek to rescind many of the Title IX changes enacted during the previous few years, and it looks like there will be new federal regulations issued in 2022. How these amendments will impact future cases, I cannot say at this time. My advice is to do a little research with your teens prior to sending them off to school. The more you know, the better you can help them prepare.

MY EXPERIENCE WITH TITLE IX

In Title IX cases, I would like to say it's as simple as "always believe the victim," but it isn't. Unfortunately, many cases I've been involved in include false accusations and misinterpretations on the part of the accuser. One of the first Title IX cases I was involved in concerned an appeal from a young man who was a student athlete. My client had attended a state meet where the students from his university had stayed overnight in a local hotel. The following facts were agreed upon by both my client and the complainant in their statements and in their testimony at the hearing:

In their hotel room that night, my client and his roommate were hanging out with a few people. One of them was the complainant, a woman who lay down under the covers in my client's bed during the gathering. When everyone else left a few hours later, this woman stayed in my client's bed. My client said that he lay down on the bed above the covers and attempted to go to sleep. She invited him under the covers. One thing led to another, and they started kissing and touching each other. She suggested going into the bathroom, where they engaged in intercourse. During this time, my client's roommate was in the room, asleep in the other bed. After the activity in the bathroom, my client and this woman then slept in the same bed. In the morning, she got up, said goodbye to him and his roommate, and they parted ways.

Twenty months later, my client received notice that the school was bringing him up on a Title IX charge. The woman was accusing my client of not having secured her affirmative consent to have intercourse. While she agreed with the sequence of events reported above, she added that once they had gone into the bathroom, she had not given my client affirmative consent to have intercourse through her words or her actions.

My client was dumbfounded. She had suggested going into the bathroom so they wouldn't wake the roommate. She hadn't shown any signs of wanting him not to proceed. If the woman had felt violated, why hadn't she stopped the activity? Why hadn't she told him she didn't want to have intercourse? Why had she spent the night in his bed with him afterward? Why hadn't she reached out to his roommate, who was present in the room, for help? Why had she waited 20 months to make the complaint?

My client consulted family and friends prior to the hearing. He told them what happened and every one of them had the same reaction—they didn't understand the affirmative consent standard, so they formed their opinion about the event based on their own experiences and what they believed logically made sense. They all told him that he had done nothing wrong, and they were sure the school would agree.

My client went to the hearing, explained his story, and thought he made a convincing case for his innocence. But then he was asked specific questions by the panel with respect to the affirmative consent standard. And because he didn't understand the standards in these kinds of cases, he was not able to specifically explain *how he had obtained affirmative consent to have intercourse.* He was found responsible for nonconsensual intercourse because he was not able to show how he had received affirmative consent from the complainant. He was expelled from school. The fallout from what he had perceived to be an "innocent hook-up" bulldozed his education and his future. Fortunately, after this incident, the student consulted with me, and we were able to appeal and have a new panel hear the case again. While he was still found responsible, the new panel better understood his actions and put him on probation, which allowed him to stay in school and not have a permanent mark in his transcript.

This young man and his family were confident that he would be found not responsible because their "common sense" told them he hadn't done anything wrong. But they didn't completely understand the process. I've seen these cases time and time again and want to help you so you and your kid can avoid similar situations. Title IX charges cannot be evaluated using common sense or by comparing the situation to how things were when you were in college. College students must be aware that "affirmative consent" must be obtained for each and every sexual act they participate in with their partner. They must be able to detail their partner's verbal and physical responses to show a clear willingness to participate in the sexual activity.

FALLOUT FROM TITLE IX CASES

With a permanent Title IX mark on a transcript, a child will not only have difficulty getting a good education but getting a job where he'll need to provide a college transcript. And, whether convicted or not, a student may be branded in his social circle and online as a sexual predator. This branding can have lifelong psychological and other consequences.

I have represented students who knowingly did not abide by the affirmative consent standard and subsequently received a conviction and a punishment that fit their unacceptable actions. The great majority of students I've represented, however, were terrified kids who had no idea how they got into such a situation. Yes, the prevailing perception is that false accusations are rare. However, in my experience as a lawyer, they are common enough that I feel it is imperative that parents address the issue with their teens.

Consider these nebulous cases where a student's reputation and future were on the line:

- I represented a client who was accused of coercing his girlfriend into sex. The only factor that constituted coercion in her testimony was that she attested that my client would have made her feel guilty if she didn't have sex with him.

- I represented a student whose partner claimed he could penetrate her three times during intercourse. He went in and out six times, thus technically violating the limits set on affirmative consent.

- A girl claimed she was too drunk to remember having intercourse and accused my client of taking advantage of her in her inebriated state. The problem was that her suitemates testified that, minutes before intercourse, she had a completely coherent conversation with them, detailing how excited she was to have sex with my client.

- One of my clients had a woman accuse him a month after having intercourse of not gaining consent. This was confusing to my client, as the woman had sent a text after the incident affirming that she had enjoyed their time together and hoped to be with him intimately again. However, we showed at the hearing that she had a boyfriend at the time of the incident; after the boyfriend found out, he told others that she had cheated on him. That is when the woman filed charges against my client.

Each of these students was accused of not receiving affirmative consent from their accuser before a sexual interaction. I was able to show at each of these hearings that my client *did* receive affirmative consent; all of them were found not responsible for non-consensual sexual activity in violation of Title IX. We were able to provide evidence of affirmative consent; and I was able to successfully show the credibility of each of my clients' stories and why the complainant's story in each case just didn't make sense.

KNOW THE SEXUAL MISCONDUCT POLICY

The most important information you can give your child is awareness of their school's sexual misconduct policy before they become intimately involved with another student. This goes for females and males. While the criminal justice system punishes those convicted of sexual assault, the federal government encourages schools to implement their own disciplinary procedures and punishment for offenders. This could include suspension, a mark on one's permanent record, or even expulsion.

The standard at most schools is "Was there affirmative consent for the sexual act?" Here is an example of a typical "affirmative consent" definition in a university Code of Conduct:

Affirmative consent is a knowing, voluntary, and mutual decision among all participants to engage in sexual activity. Consent can be given by words or actions, as long as those words or actions create clear permission regarding willingness to engage in the sexual activity. Silence or lack of resistance, in and of itself, does not demonstrate consent. The definition of consent does not vary based upon a participant's sex, sexual orientation, gender identity, or gender expression.

Non-consent/Limitations of Consent

i.   Consent to any sexual contact or any specific sexual act cannot be given if an individual is under the age of 17.

ii. Consent to any sexual act or prior consensual sexual activity between or with any party does not necessarily constitute consent to any other sexual act.

iii. Consent to engage in sexual activity with one person does not imply consent to engage in sexual activity with any other person.

iv. Consent is required regardless of whether the person initiating the act is under the influence of drugs and/or alcohol.

v.   Consent cannot be given when a person is incapacitated, which occurs when an individual lacks the ability to knowingly choose to participate in sexual activity. Incapacitation may be caused by:

    a. A physical or mental condition, infirmity or disability that limited informed decision making;

    b. The lack of consciousness or being asleep;

    c. Being involuntarily restrained; or

    d. If an individual otherwise cannot consent.

Depending on the degree of intoxication, someone who is under the influence of alcohol, drugs, or other intoxicants (whether involuntary or voluntary) may be incapacitated and therefore unable to consent.

    a. Consent cannot be given when it is the result of any coercion, intimidation, force, or threat of immediate or future harm.

    b. Coercion is the use of an unreasonable amount of pressure to engage in sexual activity. Coercion is more than an effort to persuade, entice, or attract another person to engage in sexual activity.

    c. Intimidation is an implied threat that menaces or causes reasonable fear in another person.

vii. Consent cannot be given when it is the result of the use of physical intimidation to secure compliance with sexual activity.

viii. Intoxication or impairment of the Respondent is no defense to charges of sexual misconduct.

140

Revocation of Consent

i.   Consent may be initially given, but it may be revoked/or withdrawn at any time, either verbally, through physical resistance, or by losing consciousness.

ii. When consent is withdrawn or cannot be given, sexual activity must stop.

iii. Failure to cease sexual contact promptly in response to withdrawal of consent constitutes prohibited non-consensual sexual contact.[56]

Again, this is only one example from one university. It's important for your teen to know what applies at their school.

ADVICE FOR PARENTS AND TEENS

No parent wants their child to be a victim of sexual misconduct. No parent wants their child to be accused of a Title IX violation, either. That's why it's important to teach both our daughters and our sons to be smart. Teach young men and women to respect each other and to take the steps to ensure their partners feel safe and respected. Sure, it may not be sexy in the moment to ask, "Can I touch you here?" but it is the right thing to do and could be what saves them in the future. Students must understand that they must receive affirmative consent at each and every step during a sexual interaction. They must understand that an incapacitated partner cannot ever give consent; they must also understand that their partner may revoke consent at any time, and, at that point, they must cease all activity. Teach young men and women to take ownership of their intimacy and, if they are in a situation where they feel uncomfortable, they should speak up right away and do whatever they can to extricate themselves from the situation (even if that means a kick or punch).

Should your teen ever be accused, hire a lawyer right away and make sure no statement is provided prior to counsel. A school administration is not looking out for your child's best interest. Just because you pay tuition does not mean they will hesitate to act. As far as most schools are concerned, losing one student's tuition is better than potentially losing federal funding.

Again, talk to your kids about Title IX. It might not be comfortable, but it could save you and them a great deal of pain.

CHAPTER 18

The college disciplinary process

When students are charged with a violation of their school's Code of Conduct, they often don't understand the seriousness of the situation until it is too late to help themselves. Colleges give the illusion that they are on the student's side but, when suspension or expulsion is on the line, the accused student can feel left in the lurch.

In this chapter, we'll go over some common college infractions that merit hearings, as well as the college hearing procedure from complaint to hearing to punishment.

INFRACTIONS THAT ARE GROUNDS FOR DISCIPLINE
So, how does a college kid find himself at one of these hearings in the first place? We've discussed the most common infractions that get college students in trouble: throwing a kegger in the sorority house, smoking pot on the front steps of the dormitory, paying a roommate for his old political science paper from last quarter, etc. However, students can get in trouble for many other things that merit academic hearings. Most likely, these are all listed in the student Code of Conduct handbook; but since most students and parents do not read the handbook, here are some common offenses you and your teen should know about:

- **Having illegal substances (other than alcohol or drugs) in the room,** such as candles, rice cookers, toaster ovens, humidifiers, samurai swords, gasoline, scooters, water beds, and generators, to name a few.

- **"Covering" for other students.** I once had a client who was covering attendance for six other students. The school used a "beeper" system to sign in to class, and a faculty member saw that this kid had seven beepers in front of him. There was really no arguing that charge.

- **Pranks.** In college, we used to put baby powder under the door and use a blow dryer to blow it into someone's room. Did you know that baby powder is combustible? Fortunately for us, our pranks never ended in a *kaboom*. But, given the right variables, this could have been a terrible situation. So many kids get busted for a simple prank gone wrong.

- **Damaging school property.** A student gets mad and punches a hole in a wall or, in a drunken stupor, steals a sign to hang on the dorm room wall. To a kid, these might just seem like harmless antics, but to college administrators this damage to school property could be grounds for suspension.

- **Possessing a weapon.** A kid might think it's funny to wave around his new ninja stars, but this is actually a serious offense, especially if someone feels threatened by said ninja stars.

- **Harassment and bullying.** With the proliferation of social media, it is so easy to bully classmates. And, as we covered in an earlier chapter, it is also very easy to get caught.

- **Stalking.** A kid might think it's cute to follow around the pretty girl from Organic Chemistry 101. It's not. Chances are, she doesn't think so, either.

- **Pulling the fire alarm.** It's not just a harmless prank. It's surprisingly expensive and a waste of time and energy for all school officials involved.

- **Trespassing on school property.** Think it's funny to sneak into the science lab at 2 a.m.? College administrators don't, and they have you on camera.

What happens when a student is accused of violating the school's Code of Conduct?

THE PROCESS
Typically, the college hearing process is as follows:

- Complaint

- Notice

- Pre-hearing process

- Hearing

- Punishment

- Appeal (Optional)

Complaint

The process almost always starts when someone makes a complaint to a professor, guidance counselor, RA, or even the police. No matter who receives the complaint, it will usually end up in the hands of the Office of Student Conduct (or a similar department or group on campus). From there, the Office of Student Conduct does an official investigation, during which they compile evidence via interviews with those involved and gather any physical evidence and on-campus security footage. Sometimes students are notified during the investigation stage; sometimes they are not (If the school asks to speak with a student at this stage, the rules I outline later in the chapter should be followed). If the Office of Student Conduct determines that they believe that someone has committed an offense, they'll move forward with a disciplinary case.

Notice

When the Office of Student Conduct decides to move forward with a disciplinary case against a student, they must give the student notice and send an email or letter to let him know they are charging him. Typically, this notification will request that the student come into the office to discuss the charge. In almost all instances, the school will NOT notify the parents or legal guardians of the accused student.

Pre-Hearing Process

In the initial meeting with a student, school officials may do the following:

1. Explain the disciplinary process to the student and what to expect going forward.

2. Try to interrogate the student and solicit a confession.

3. Say, "Hey, this is what you're charged with and if you want to take responsibility, this is the punishment. If you sign this waiver

146

of your right to a hearing, we'll administer the punishment, and this doesn't have to go any further."

It is possible that all of these topics will be covered in a single meeting, or they may be covered in three separate meetings.

If the school wants to take a statement from a student during this meeting, my advice to the student is to say something like, "I would be happy to have a meeting and listen to the allegations, but I will not make a statement until I have had time to process the information." In countless cases, I have reviewed the statements my clients made to the school *before* they hired me, and these statements were never helpful to their case. In fact, they are almost always harmful. When the end result may be suspension or expulsion, the stakes are too high for 19-year-olds to successfully talk their way out of a serious allegation via a statement (perhaps with the singular exception of one buddy of mine in college who could talk his way out of *anything*).

One more thing I'd like to point out that I've heard over and over again from clients who have been in these meetings: when explaining the disciplinary process to the accused student, school officials often treat the accused not as the perpetrator of some terrible act but like any other student in a difficult situation. The administrator tells the nervous student that no one has made up their mind yet and affords them the opportunity to seek counseling, a class adjustment, or anything else that will help avoid disrupting their educational experience.

While I commend the schools for treating the accused in a reasonable way, I feel that it ultimately does a disservice to the student. It gives the accused students a false sense of security. "I know they said I could be suspended or expelled, but if they thought I really did something wrong, why would they offer me counseling and more time to take my finals?" At this point, many students don't grasp the seriousness of the situation. Students are often taken by surprise, then, when their hearing ends in expulsion or suspension.

The Biggest Difference Between Criminal and College Cases

On the surface, defense of a criminal charge and defense of a college disciplinary charge seem similar. Someone is accused of a bad act. There is an investigation, the person is charged, prosecuted, and the case moves toward a resolution. But the actual procedure of these two systems couldn't be more different.

When representing a client in a criminal case, I deal with the prosecutor, who represents the government. The prosecutor will evaluate her evidence and determine if she has a strong case against my client or if there are evidence issues. She will take into consideration the complainant's thoughts about resolving the matter. She will also take into consideration the information I provide about my client's intent and his good character. She considers all of this information and determines what she believes is a fair result. When we discuss the case, we both typically are motivated to come to a resolution. Once we agree, we discuss it with the judge; if my client agrees, we move forward with a disposition. If the prosecutor and I cannot reach an agreement, then we move forward to trial. My goal is to negotiate with the prosecutor and judge to secure a disposition that will create the fewest ramifications for my client. The great majority of cases are resolved without going to trial.

When a student is charged with a violation of a school's Code of Conduct, the initial procedure is similar to a criminal case. There is a "bad act," an investigation, then charges are brought. The difference in a school case is that no one at the school is considered the "prosecutor." Someone might have conducted an investigation. Someone might be assigned the case by the Student Conduct Office who could explain to you and your kid the process and answer any questions. However, no one from the school will evaluate the case and engage in discussions toward finding a resolution.

The school will let the student know that if she takes responsibility, there will be a specific punishment, but the school will not entertain a conversation or negotiation with regards to the finding or to moderating the punishment. So, unless the student agrees to the resolution and punishment the school recommends, there will be a hearing. In criminal cases, as noted, an extremely small percentage of cases go to trial. Almost all school disciplinary cases go to a hearing.

Hearing

The actual procedure for the hearing can vary wildly. Sometimes it's not really a hearing but the student sitting in a room with an administrator and explaining why she shouldn't be found responsible and, after a 15-minute meeting, that administrator makes a decision. Sometimes it's a meeting with a panel consisting of staff and students. Sometimes the school simply wants the accused student to give a statement. Sometimes the school wants to conduct a full-blown hearing including opening statements, witness testimonies, cross-examinations, and summations.

Here's the kicker, though: whatever the type of hearing procedure, students must always represent *themselves*. Sometimes a student's lawyer will be allowed in the room, sometimes not. Either way, lawyers are not allowed to represent the student in the room. Other than cross-examining witnesses in Title IX procedures, the lawyer acts as the student's advisor and is *not* the one making the oral arguments. To me, this part of the process is unfair. While there are instances when an accused student is charismatic and can charm the pants off the panel, at other times an accused student is an introvert who might stumble over his words when he's nervous. Obviously, the charming student has a distinct advantage.

I remember one case in which my client was terrified and had trouble communicating to the panel. I had prepared a statement for him, and we had practiced numerous times. At the hearing, he spoke in a low, meek voice and did not make eye contact with anyone. He stuttered and repeated words. All I wanted to do was jump in and make the arguments for him to the panel, but I could not. The poor kid started with a huge disadvantage.

But having a lawyer is still necessary in these cases. When I represent a student, I put together, with their help, statements and arguments for the hearing. I prepare them for questions from the complainant and the panel and train them as best I can to successfully defend themselves. Truthfully, unless a student hires a lawyer like me to help them craft their argument, most of the time their argument amounts to something akin to, "I didn't do it. Please don't ruin my life." Saying "I didn't do it" is never enough. The student has to argue why a case can't be proven. And it is unreasonable to ask 18-year-olds to make coherent arguments on the level that I, as a lawyer of 20-plus years, have made for countless clients.

At this point, you may be wondering why the school hearing process is so different from the criminal trial process. The reason is that college students aren't entitled to the same due process as they are when dealing with the criminal courts. School is considered a "property right," not a "liberty right." Examples of liberty rights include freedom of speech, freedom of the press, and the right to privacy. Examples of property rights include the right to own possessions, the right to ownership of animals, the right to ownership of intellectual property, and, of course, the right to a higher-level education.

Taking away property rights does not impede your liberty. And, although both you and I know that hampering a kid's college education can have a significant impact on the rest of that kid's life, education is still seen as a privilege. Thus, schools do not have to abide by the same due process, since suspension or expulsion is not considered as severe as limiting access to liberty rights.

Punishment
A final decision typically is not made at the time of the hearing. Usually, the panel or the administrator determining the outcome deliberates for a period of time and then renders a decision in writing. Although I'm not sure exactly what goes on behind closed doors, I assume that after the panel makes its decision, it is most likely

reviewed by higher-up administrators and the school's legal counsel before it is enacted.

When determining punishment, a panel will typically consider the student's age and maturity, the nature of the infraction, surrounding and extenuating circumstances, disabilities, prior violations, and character testimonies from people close to the accused. While punishment may vary, here are the common types:

- Warning

- Restitution for property damages

- Rehabilitative classes

- Restrictions on certain events and participation in clubs or athletic teams

- Probation

- Community service

- Probation, suspension, or expulsion from dormitories

- Reassignment to different on-campus residences or classes

- Prohibiting contact with accusing parties

- Final probation (if found responsible for additional offense, student will be automatically suspended)

- Suspension

- Expulsion

Keep in mind that punishments can vary widely among schools. What is a relatively minor violation at one school could be considered a significant violation at another. Students should know their school's policy and culture.

Appeal

If the student loses the case and wants to appeal, there are three instances in which they may appeal:

1. New evidence comes to light.

2. The school violated the hearing procedures or their own standards as outlined in their Code of Conduct. (The Code of Conduct is a contract not only for the students but for the school as well.)

3. The punishment is not reasonable, given the offense.

In all cases, the student must submit a written request for an appeal within a given time period (usually a few days to a few weeks). If the student didn't have a lawyer the first time around, I highly recommend one for the appeal.

While some schools have two levels of appeal, after the final appeal to the school, there is no higher entity before which to plead the case beyond the courts. And while students can choose to sue the school, there must be a clear legal wrong that the court can right. Also consider that courts traditionally give schools wide latitude to implement their own rules. That said, there are cases when suing the school is a reasonable option. For example:

I had a case when a client was convicted of a Title IX offense in April of his senior year, after he had already taken his finals. The school refused to give him credit for his final semester, even though he had technically completed the semester. To redo the semester to complete his college education, he would have needed to transfer (which isn't easy with a Title IX offense on the transcript). By sending the school a "Demand Letter" and detailing the reasons we felt we would be successful with a civil suit, my client and I were able to get the school to agree that he had completed his classes and that the school must assign credit for them.

A college hearing can be overwhelming no matter who the student is or where they are in their academic career. My advice to any college student in this situation is to research, prepare their argument, and hire a lawyer if they are facing a penalty that could have a seriously negative effect on their life.

CHAPTER 19

Helping students with disabilities

Although this topic might not seem to belong in a book about how kids get into trouble, there is a connection that makes sense. When my youngest daughter was in second grade, I learned about education law and practiced it for a few years. During that time, I noticed that many of the kids who were getting in trouble in school had a recognized or an unrecognized disability. I also noticed that most parents didn't understand much about how the schools could help their child. So, I'm offering here a brief overview of the process. (If you are in this situation and need more in-depth information, check out the book I mention later in the chapter.)

Did you know that 14 percent of all public-school students aged 3 to 21 receive government-mandated special education services?[57] When I was a kid, special education was a place, a separate classroom, where the kids with severe disabilities were boxed up, away from the rest of the student population. It was imprisonment. Punishment for being different.

Nowadays, thankfully, we know better. Kids can struggle with different kinds of disabilities—mental, physical, emotional, and social. Each of these disabilities comes with its own obstacles, and the educational system has slowly but surely found ways to address these obstacles via Individualized Education Programs (IEP). These programs include publicly available services to help students with disabilities get the most out of their education, including behavioral modification, speech therapy, classroom modifications, added testing time, and more.

But I know through personal experience and my experience as a lawyer that many schools are still reluctant to commit to IEPs for students.

The reason I raise this subject in the context of this book is because I see many kids and even older clients who have disabilities. I believe if the school or the parents had advocated for them to be evaluated and given the proper supports and modifications to their education earlier on in their lives, these students may never have found themselves sitting in my office.

In this chapter, we'll discuss how to get help from the school system for students with disabilities—help that they need and that they rightfully deserve.

MY OWN EXPERIENCE

When my youngest daughter was in second grade, her teacher mentioned to my wife and me that she was struggling with reading and suggested we have her evaluated. We had noticed our daughter's difficulties and decided to follow her teacher's advice. After the evaluation, we went to a meeting with the Committee on Special Education (CSE) and were told that our daughter did not have a disability. My wife and I were relieved, but our daughter continued to struggle. We realized we needed to make sure she was receiving the education she needed.

My wife and I decided to have our daughter privately evaluated. Guess what? After their thorough evaluation, they determined our daughter *was* struggling with a disability. They provided a detailed report on how the school could help her. I did my research and learned that having a student evaluated and determining eligibility for special education programs are actually legal issues, and that the school was required, by law, to accommodate my daughter's special needs.

We scheduled another meeting with the school. This time, I told the school administrators that I was coming in as a lawyer, not as a parent. In the end, my daughter got the help she needed (and was legally entitled to!). Had I not done my own research and understood the legal issues, had we not consulted outside evaluators, had our daughter's second-grade teacher not been kind enough to reach out to my wife and me, had I not approached the second meeting with the school with a lawyer's mindset, my daughter might still struggle today. Happily, the modifications and supports that were put in place for her were truly life-changing. Today, I am proud to say my daughter is a successful college student with a bright future ahead.

Because of my experience, I deeply empathize with parents of kids who have, or whom they suspect to have, disabilities. I want to help you help your kid, too.

HOW TO REQUEST AN EVALUATION

Every child is entitled by law to an appropriate education. According to the 1975 Individuals with Disabilities Education Act (IDEA), all students aged 3 to 21 determined by a team of professionals to have a disability that impacts academic education and performance are entitled to an appropriate education that accommodates their special needs.[58]

Here's a harsh reality: If your kid has a disability, especially if it is undiagnosed and untreated, he *will* struggle in school. If you suspect your child has a disability, I highly recommend asking the school to have him evaluated. While my wife and I were fortunate that our daughter's teacher saw that she was struggling and recommended the intervention, this is not common. Do not expect your school to say, "Hey, we think your child needs to be evaluated." Some will. Most will not. It is unfortunate, but it is incumbent upon parents to recognize the issue and to act when their child is struggling.

To request an evaluation, be sure to review the rules in your school district. Typically, parents must send a letter to the school district's Board of Education and explicitly request that their child be evaluated for a disability. This step is essential to ensure that the school takes action to evaluate your child.

Be prepared for the possibility that the school will fight you about getting an evaluation. Due to budget constraints, schools don't make a habit of telling parents to have their child evaluated, nor do they encourage evaluations. Simply put, the cost of educating a child with a disability is higher than educating a child without a disability. There are even school districts that will do everything in their power not to explain what the schools are required by law to provide and what your and your child's rights are.

As parents, it can sometimes be difficult to challenge your kid's school, because it holds a special place in your community. It is the place you trust to help your most loved human grow and develop. You spend countless hours at parent-teacher nights, school plays, and field days. You have nothing but great things to say about the people shepherding your children's education. Because of that, many parents mistakenly assume that school officials always have the kids' best interests at heart. As a parent who has been through this process, and as a lawyer who has dealt with too many cases where the kid didn't get the help he needed, I can tell you this isn't always true.

In cases where you encounter resistance from your child's school (and for anyone who thinks their child may have a disability), my best recommendation is to educate yourself about the process. I would specifically recommend reading *Wrightslaw: From Emotions to Advocacy: The Special Education Survival Guide, 2nd Edition.*[59] Knowledge is the best way to fight for your child's future.

WHAT HAPPENS AFTER THE EVALUATION

After the evaluation (either by the school or by an independent evaluator), the school will schedule a meeting with the CSE team and the parent to discuss the results of the evaluation and, if need be, develop an IEP with the proper support and interventions to provide the best education for your child. This is very important: do not just give the results of a private evaluation to your school and expect them to act without having a CSE meeting. Here's a case to illustrate:

I once had a client, a junior in high school, who faced disciplinary issue after disciplinary issue. She was also struggling academically. I asked the mother if she'd ever had her daughter evaluated. She responded that she and her husband had had her privately evaluated in the eighth grade. They had given the results of the evaluation, which showed an obvious disability, to the high school guidance counselor, who said, "Okay, we'll take care of it." Guess what? The school didn't. The parents assumed the school was taking action to help their daughter; they had no idea about the steps they would have needed to take to ensure their daughter received her IEP. No one had told the parents that they had to make a request to the district for a review and also make a formal request for special education services via a CSE meeting.

Be warned that, as with an evaluation, your child's school may actively try to dissuade you from pursuing an IEP. It is important that you come to CSE meetings prepared with a goal for what you want to get out of it. In my experience with these meetings, the group will review the evaluation and take so long doing so that, by the time they're done, there is little time to discuss a concrete plan of action for your child. My advice for parents is to take control of the conversation from the outset. Set the tone by saying something like, "I understand you need to go through certain issues, but I have a number of issues I would like to discuss, and I would like to make sure we have time to do so."

Another tactic school officials may try is to ask, "Well, what do you think we should do?" While it is important for parents to have some knowledge, it is not the parent's job to know the ins and outs of special education programs. Schools know what steps they can take, and it is fully within your power to require that they take those steps. Be clear with school officials. You can say firmly but kindly: "You owe my child an appropriate education. What are you going to do about it? You have the expertise. Please help my child and my family to the best of your ability." Once parents how the process works, it is easier to get the school to do what you want. It's getting to that point that is the real challenge.

Be aware that if your child is given an IEP, she will be re-evaluated in years to come, and you will need to repeat this process of meeting with school administrators every year. Hold on to your power, however, and you should be all right. Adopt that "lawyer's mindset."

All warnings aside, know that some schools are supportive of children with disabilities and will go the extra mile to help their students succeed. I see the worst cases, and I have cultivated a hardline approach here simply because I want to ensure that your child does not fall victim to a sometimes-flawed system.

One more note: Colleges don't typically treat disabilities the same way that high schools do. While some colleges do provide accommodations, it is a much different process than in public secondary school, where you are guaranteed the right to an appropriate education. If your college-age child has a disability, and you feel he may need some sort of accommodation or intervention, before deciding, it is best to evaluate each school's supports. Some schools have excellent disability services, and some do not. You will want to thoroughly research the supports at potential college picks to give your child the best opportunity to thrive in their academic environment now and in any future educational pursuits.

A FEW FINAL WORDS ON IEPS

While I am passionate about getting kids the help they deserve, note that this discussion does not pertain to parents and kids who abuse the system. For example, there are parents who claim their child has a "disability" for the first time in tenth grade because they want their kid to get time-and-a-half while taking the SAT. I do not in any way condone abuse of a system that is already limited. This chapter solely concerns kids with diagnosable issues that can genuinely be helped by an IEP intervention. If that is true for your child, then I urge you to take my advice and give him his best shot at a good education.

CHAPTER 20

What breaking the rules means for your kid's future

Suppose the courts or a school finds a teen responsible for a violation or crime. What then? What does that mean for that teen going forward?

Since the mid-1990s, school disciplinary action has skyrocketed, leaving many students and their parents in fear for the student's future. A report conducted by the Center for Community Alternatives (CCA) found that a whopping 3 million students are suspended each year, and 100,000 more are expelled.[60] These punishments lead to a higher probability of dropout, decreased graduation rates, a greater chance of subsequent involvement in criminal activity, and fewer educational, career, and housing opportunities.

In this chapter, we'll explore how conviction in high school, college, and by the criminal courts can affect a child's future.

THE FUTURE AFTER HIGH SCHOOL INFRACTIONS

The primary concern for students who are convicted of high school disciplinary offenses is the impact on their college applications.

Realistically, there are few ramifications beyond college applications, other than possibly seeking employment with a government agency. Therefore, I'm going to focus on how high school infractions impact college applications.

How much do colleges really care about infractions in high school? Unfortunately, the numbers show that they care *a lot*. According to the aforementioned CCA Report, 73 percent of colleges collect applicant disciplinary history and 89 percent of those use that information to determine admission. Added to that, if they do admit the student, 34 percent of colleges will prevent those students with high school disciplinary infractions from living on campus![61]

How do these colleges obtain the disciplinary records in the first place? Two ways: either via a direct request from the school or via direct student admission. The CCA reported that while half of high schools choose not to acquiesce to a college's request for disciplinary records, the other half does share disciplinary records, even though most of them (63 percent) lack formal written policies and guidelines about sharing such information.[62] And most of the time, a disciplinary record was reviewed only by a single guidance counselor prior to being sent to the college. This means that while it's possible that a school might conceal a convicted teen's record, it's just as likely they will make it publicly available upon request, with little review. It's critical that both you and your teen are aware of the school's policy prior to application.

So, what about self-admission of past disciplinary action? Beginning in the 2006–2007 academic year, the Common App, used by more than 500 colleges and universities nationwide, began to incorporate this question in their application:

"Have you ever been found responsible for a disciplinary violation at any educational institution you have attended from the 9th grade (or the international equivalent) forward, whether related to academic misconduct or behavioral misconduct, that resulted in a disciplinary action? These actions could include, but are not limited to: probation, suspension, removal, dismissal, or expulsion from the institution."[63]

There is no evidence that limiting admissions based on prior infractions bolsters student safety. Nevertheless, these colleges, along with many others that don't use the Common App, continue to include these questions to evaluate applicants. And while some schools that have open enrollment, such as community colleges, can't deny entrance, they can certainly limit a student's education in the interest of "public safety."

All this said, many schools won't explicitly deny admission to a student with a disciplinary record unless it is a severe case involving violence. Keep in mind, however, that students compete against other high-caliber students for admission. If both students have similar academic histories but one has a record and the other doesn't, which one do you think the college will choose?

Does this mean the student shouldn't admit on their college application that they have been convicted of a violation of their school's disciplinary code? Unfortunately, no. Since you can never be certain whether the high school has shared the disciplinary record, my advice is for the student to be honest and humble on college applications, unfair as the question may be. I recommend that students take responsibility for their mistakes and impress upon application readers that they took active steps to change their behavior.

THE FUTURE AFTER COLLEGE INFRACTIONS

College infractions have the potential to be much more detrimental to a student's future than those incurred in high school. Not only can they impact future education but they can result in limitations on future employment and can harm one's reputation.

Note, however, that colleges vary widely as to the content of transcripts. Some will keep suspensions on the transcript; some will not. Some will record expulsions, but then expunge the record after a period of time. Some will let students appeal a permanent transcript mark; some will not. Again, know *your* kid's school policy.

For example, here is the policy from New Jersey's Rutgers University:[64]

- Disciplinary records are retained by the Office of Student Conduct for each student who violates conduct.

- Unless the student was dismissed from the university, these records are destroyed after 10 years.

- Expulsion records are retained indefinitely.

- Access to conduct records requires a release authorization.

- Records of conduct are retained separately from transcripts.

- Conduct violations are added to transcripts.

- Suspensions are removed from transcripts after they end.

- Expulsions remain on the transcript unless clemency is obtained.

- Students may apply for clemency of expulsion records after five years.

Some states also mandate that schools adhere to state laws. For example, New York mandates that if a student is found responsible for a Title IX offense and consequently suspended or expelled, this information must go on the transcript. And, believe me, a mark on a transcript citing expulsion for a Title IX violation is not something a person wants to explain when applying to another school or for a job.

If a school doesn't record infractions on a student's permanent record, should the student admit it? Unfortunately, as with high school infractions, my answer is yes. Even if it doesn't show up on the transcript, even if the student can appeal to get their record expunged, the question is whether they have been *found responsible*, not whether it is on their record.

It also may easily be deduced. For example, say the transcript shows that they went to State University for four semesters, then community college for a semester, then back to State University. Most employers are rightfully suspicious of what this indicates, which is why it is important to be truthful about a disruption in education.

THE FUTURE AFTER CRIMINAL CONVICTIONS

Criminal convictions are a whole other ballgame. Criminal convictions are recorded by one's fingerprints. This means that whenever someone does a background check, usually they contact a centralized state bureau, which provides all information on any convictions in the student's state for misdemeanor and felony charges (this does *not* include records for non-criminal charges or dismissals). People conduct background checks for a variety of reasons; the information could impact future employment, housing, educational opportunities, public assistance, and state and federal benefits. Criminal convictions may affect:

- College admissions

- FAFSA student loan eligibility

- Hope Tax Credit eligibility

- Section 8 Housing (even if the child is living with parents, a criminally offended child can be evicted)

- Job applications

- Driver's license

• CDL licenses

• Licensed professional certifications, which include careers such as barber and plumber

• Custody proceedings

• Voting rights

• Right to own or purchase firearms

• Immigration

• Right to travel

• Ability to apply to be an elected official and serve in certain other government institutions

• The right to serve on a jury

Keep in mind that different states have different policies when it comes to criminal convictions. While one offense may be a relatively minor misdemeanor in New York, it could be a serious infraction in Arkansas. Moreover, some states require transparency with current employers about previous convictions, so you and your kid should know the laws and the culture in your state when a background check is required. All this is to say: if your kid receives a criminal conviction, he should be prepared to fight for the many rights and privileges that we take for granted every day.

Another question people wonder about is, "If a student receives a criminal conviction, should they admit it to potential employers, landlords, etc.?" Absolutely. States, such as New York, regularly submit criminal records to a statewide repository. While not every state is so consistent, your kid should err on the side of caution and assume that anyone who wants to access information on prior convictions will be able to.

More than that, some people may even have access to an FBI background check, which not only shows convictions but can show pending cases and arrests that ended in non-conviction. That is a significant problem, because FBI background checks are notoriously inaccurate. Both a 2006 Department of Justice Report[65] and a 2015 U.S. Government Accountability Office study[66] showed substantial inconsistencies and inaccuracies in the system. States and counties routinely fail to report arrest records, court dispositions, and expungement records, leading to inconsistencies. This means that even if a record is sealed or expunged, if someone does an FBI background check, the allegedly expunged offense might still be visible.

It is unfortunate that kids who have a single immature moment or make one bad decision can face a lifetime of consequences. Many kids simply don't have the capacity to understand that their actions can have such drastic consequences. But knowing what challenges your kids are facing is half the battle. If they are prepared, honest, and take responsibility for any convictions, they have a fighting chance for their future.

CONCLUSION: BE SMART

If I can leave you with one all-encompassing lesson to impart to your kids, it is to **be smart**. In every choice your teen makes, she is learning what it means to be an adult. And becoming an adult means knowing when to keep your mouth closed, when to say something, and, most important, when to reach out for help when you need it.

I wrote this book because I remember the feeling of being young and dumb and a bit out of control. Harkening back to my college brush with the school authorities and the police at the beginning of this book, I remember being terrified sitting at the precinct while the police accused me of lying. I was astonished that they wanted me to sign a statement that wasn't true. I was enraged that the school charged me even after the police arrested the real perpetrator. I believed my actions were reasonable. I simply wanted to tell the police and the school the truth. I wanted people to *listen* to me. But the police just wanted to close their case. The school just wanted me to do what they said.

What I didn't understand then, and what I want to help you and your kids to understand now, is that my expectations were vastly different from the way the law actually works. The legal and school systems today aren't designed to be on the side of the accused. In my career, I've made no bones about it: this process frustrates me. In many ways, I feel the system can be deeply unfair toward young, developing people who have no grasp of the weight their actions carry. I wish colleges allowed students to hire attorneys to fully represent them. I wish all school districts understood that smoking a joint is not a good reason to suspend a kid for six months. I wish cops knew that interrogating a 16-year-old scared out of her mind is different from questioning a 54-year-old who has had experience dealing with high-pressure situations. But I can't change those things.

What I can do is help you and your teen through these tough situations. I can help warn you. I can help prevent mishaps. I can help you teach your teen how to be smart. And I want to help anyone in this situation. I don't want these kids to be forever behind the eight ball in life because of one bad judgment. One mistake.

As noted, I think my freshman-year ordeal was when my interest in law began. The jarring circumstances I found myself in for those few days are why I'm so passionate today about helping kids and their parents navigate a daunting and overwhelming legal system. I want to be the advocate I didn't have when I was that age. I want those scared families to know that someone is on their side. As a former teen, and as a parent now, I see you, and I hope this book can be a light through those dark times.

Be smart.

REFERENCES

1 Julia A. Martinez, Patricia C. Rutledge, and Kenneth J. Shur, "Fake ID Ownership and Heavy Drinking in Underage College Students: Prospective Findings," *Psychology of Addictive Behaviors*, 21(2), (2007): 226–32, https://dx.doi.org/10.1037%2F0893-164X.21.2.226; Cameron Knight, "Thousands of Fake Ids from China and Hong Kong Were Seized in Cincinnati in 2020," *Cincinnati Enquirer*, January 5, 2021, https://www.cincinnati.com/story/news/2021/01/05/ thousands-fake-ids-were-seized-cincinnati-2020/4138723001/.

2 National Minimum Drinking Age, 23 US Code § 158.

3 Knight, "Thousands of Fake IDs."

4 "Underage Drinking," US Centers for Disease Control and Prevention, October 23, 2020, https://www.cdc.gov/alcohol/fact-sheets/underage-drinking.htm.

5 *Key Substance Abuse and Mental Health Indicators in the United States: Results from the 2017 National Survey on Drug Use and Health*, US Substance Abuse and Mental Health Services Administration, September 2018, https://www.samhsa.gov/data/sites/default/files/cbhsq-reports/ NSDUHFFR2017/NSDUHFFR2017.pdf.

6 T. E. McMorrow, "In Not-Guilty Finding, Judge Faults 'Weak' Social Host Law," *The East Hampton Star*, April 11, 2018, https://www.easthamptonstar.com/police-courts/2019-05-23/ not-guilty-finding-judge-faults-weak-social-host-law.

7 National Highway Traffic Safety Administration, "Fatal Crashes Involving Young Drivers," Traffic Safety Facts Research Note DOT HS 811 218, November 2009, accessed February 11, 2021, https://crashstats.nhtsa.dot.gov/Api/Public/ViewPublication/811218.

8 "Traffic Safety Facts 2017: Alcohol-Impaired Driving," National Highway Traffic Safety Administration, November 2018, https://crashstats.nhtsa.dot.gov/Api/Public/ViewPublication/812630.

9 MADD 5th Anniversary Report to the Nation, 2011. http://www.madd.org/books/statereport/#/4/

10 National Highway Traffic Safety Administration, "Alcohol Impaired Driving," Traffic Safety Facts 2008 Data DOT HS 811 155, accessed February 11, 2021, https://crashstats.nhtsa. dot.gov/Api/Public/ViewPublication/811155

11 "Crime in the United States: 2014," Federal Bureau of Investigation, https://www.fbi.gov/ about-us/cjis/ucr/crime-in-the-u.s/2014/crime-in-the-u.s.-2014/tables/table-29; Centers for Disease Control and Prevention, "Alcohol-Impaired Driving Among Adults—United States, 2012," Morbidity and Mortality Weekly Report, August 7, 2015, http://www.cdc.gov/mmwr/ preview/mmwrhtml/mm6430a2.htm

12 Traffic Safety Facts 2013: Overview," National Highway Traffic Safety Administration, July 2015, https://crashstats.nhtsa.dot.gov/Api/Public/ViewPublication/812169.

13 "DUI Costs and Car Insurance," DMV.ORG, accessed February 11, 2021, https://www.dmv. org/insurance/dui-costs-and-car-insurance.php.

14 Michelle Megna, "How Long Does a DWI Stay on Your New York Record?" CarInsurance. com, January 20, 2013, https://www.carinsurance.com/dwi-dwai-new-york.aspx.

15 Liberty Vittert, "Opinion: Here's What the Numbers Show about the Impact of Legal Marijuana," MarketWatch, April 19, 2019, https://www.marketwatch.com/story/heres-what-the-numbers-show-about-the-impact-of-legalizing-marijuana-2019-04-09.

16 Guohua Li, Joanne E. Brady, and Qixuan Chen, "Drug Use and Fatal Motor Vehicle Crashes: A Case-Control Study," *Accident Analysis & Prevention*, 60 (2013): 205–10, https://doi. org/10.1016/j.aap.2013.09.001.

17 R. K. Jones, D. Shinar, and J. M. Walsh, *State of Knowledge of Drug-Impaired Driving*, US Department of Transportation, National Highway Traffic Safety Administration, September 2003, https://rosap.ntl.bts.gov/view/dot/1722.

18 Lauren Villa, "The Great Debate: Alcohol vs Marijuana," American Addiction Centers, November 3, 2020, https://drugabuse.com/blog/marijuana-vs-alcohol/.

19 "Is It Possible to 'Overdose' or Have a 'Bad Reaction' to Marijuana?" Centers for Disease Control and Prevention, March 7, 2018, https://www.cdc.gov/marijuana/faqs/overdose-bad-reaction.html.

20 "Marijuana Drug Facts," US National Institute on Drug Abuse, December 2019, https:// www.drugabuse.gov/publications/drugfacts/marijuana.

21 Wayne Hall, "What Has Research Over the Past Two Decades Revealed about the Adverse Health Effects of Recreational Cannabis Use?" *Addiction*, 110 (2015): 19–35, https://doi. org/10.1111/add.12703.

22 "Outbreak of Lung Injury Associated with the Use of E-Cigarette, or Vaping, Products," Centers for Disease Control and Prevention, November 27, 2020, https://www.cdc.gov/tobacco/ basic_information/e-cigarettes/severe-lung-disease.html#map-cases.

23 "Vaping Linked to COVID-19 Risk in Teens and Young Adults," News Center, accessed February 11, 2021, https://med.stanford.edu/news/all-news/2020/08/vaping-linked-to-covid-19-risk-in-teens-and-young-adults.html.

24 "NJ Woman, who was Allegedly Texting while Driving, Gets 5 Years in Prison in Pedestrian's Death," ABC7, August 22, 2020, https://abc7ny.com/texting-and-driving-distracted-pedestrian-death-alexandra-mansonet/6383478/.

25 "Distracted Driving," National Highway Traffic Safety Administration, accessed January 12, 2021, https://www.nhtsa.gov/risky-driving/distracted-driving.

26 "Teen Driver Car Accident Statistics & Facts," Edgar Snyder, May 1, 2020, https://www. edgarsnyder.com/car-accident/who-was-injured/teen/teen-driving-statistics.html.

27 Li Li, Ruth A. Shults, Rebecca R. Andridge, Merissa A. Yellman, Henry Xiang, and Motao Zhu, "Texting/Emailing While Driving Among High School Students in 35 States, United States, 2015," *Journal of Adolescent Health*, 63(6) (2018): 701–8, https://doi.org/10.1016/j.jadohealth.2018.06.010.

28 Jeff K. Caird, Katherine A. Johnston, Chelsea R. Willness, and Mark Asbridge, "The Use of Meta-Analysis or Research Synthesis to Combine Driving Simulation or Naturalistic Study Results on Driver Distraction," *Journal of Safety Research*, 49 (June 2014): 91–6, https://doi. org/10.1016/j.jsr.2014.02.013.

29 "Can Texting while Driving Lead to a Murder Charge?" hg.org, accessed February 12, 2021, https://www.hg.org/legal-articles/can-texting-while-driving-lead-to-a-murder-charge-31178.

30 Jim Jakobs, "Fresno Detective Arrested. Was Texting Before Fatal Collision with Pedestrian, Police Say," GV Wire, December 30, 2020, https://gvwire.com/2020/12/30/fresno-detective-ar-rested-was-texting-before-fatal-collision-with-pedestrian-police-say/.

31 "Distracted Driving," Governors Highway Safety Association, https://www.ghsa.org/state-laws/issues/distracted%20driving.

32 "Is It Illegal to Text at a Stop Light?" I Drive Safely, accessed February 12, 2021, https://www.idrivesafely.com/defensive-driving/trending/is-it-illegal-text-stop-light#:~:text=In%20New%20York%2C%20drivers%20of,stow%20your%20phone%20while%20driving.

33 "Intersection Safety," US Federal Highway Administration, accessed February 12, 2021, https://highways.dot.gov/research/research-programs/safety/intersection-safety.

34 Eun-Ha Choi, "Crash Factors in Intersection-Related Crashes: An On-Scene Perspective," PsycEXTRA Dataset, 2010, https://doi.org/10.1037/e621942011-001.

35 James J. Bernstein and Joseph Bernstein, "Texting at the Light and Other Forms of Device Distraction Behind the Wheel," BMC Public Health, 15 (2015): article 968, https://doi.org/10.1186/s12889-015-23-8

36 Nicholas Rizzi, "New Bill Would Ban Texting at a Red Light in New York," Sunset Park, NY Patch, July 12, 2018, https://patch.com/new-york/sunset-park/new-bill-would-ban-texting-red-light-new-york.

37 "Raise the Age (RTA)," New York State Unified Court System, accessed March 11, 2021, https://www.nycourts.gov/courthelp/Criminal/RTA.shtml.

38 "What Are Your Miranda Rights?" Miranda Warning, accessed March 25, 2021, http://www.mirandawarning.org/whatareyourmirandarights.html.

39 James Orlando, "Interrogation Techniques," Office of Legislative Research Report, Connect-icut General Assembly, accessed March 25, 2021, https://www.cga.ct.gov/2014/rpt/2014-R-0071.htm.

40 "Wicklander-Zulawski Discontinues Reid Method Instruction After More Than 30 Years," Wicklander-Zulawski & Associates, Inc., March 6, 2017, https://www.prweb.com/releases/2017/03/prweb14123356.htm.

41 New York State Law, Title 1, Article 2, Section 11, https://www.nysenate.gov/legislation/laws/EDN/11.

42 Ave Mince-Didier, "New York Sexting Laws for Teens and Minors," Nolo, October 8, 2020, https://www.criminaldefenselawyer.com/resources/teen-sexting-new-york.htm.

43 Elizabeth J. Allan, Hazing in View: College Students at Risk: Initial Findings from the National Study of Student Hazing (Collingdale, PA: DIANE Publishing, 2009).

44 Allan, E.J. and Madden, M. (2008). Hazing in view: College students at risk: Initial findings from the National Study of Student Hazing. Hazing Research and Prevention.

45 Caitlin Flanagan, "Death at a Penn State Fraternity," The Atlantic, November 9, 2017, https://www.theatlantic.com/magazine/archive/2017/11/a-death-at-penn-state/540657/.

46 "Fall Semester—A Time for Parents to Discuss the Risks of College Drinking," National Institute on Alcohol Abuse and Alcoholism, accessed March 5, 2021, https://www.niaaa.nih.gov/sites/default/files/publications/NIAAA_BacktoCollege_Fact_sheet.pdf.

47 Rachel N. Lipari and Beda Jean-François, "A Day in the Life of College Students Aged 18 to 22: Substance Use Facts," Substance Abuse and Mental Health Services Administration, accessed March 5, 2021, https://www.samhsa.gov/data/sites/default/files/report_2361/ShortReport-2361.html.

48 "Statistics," International Center for Academic Integrity, accessed March 5, 2021, https://academicintegrity.org/resources/facts-and-statistics.

49 Merriam-Webster Dictionary, s.v. "plagiarizing," accessed March 8, 2021, https://www.merriam-webster.com/dictionary/plagiarizing#note-1.

50 "More Information on Fair Use," US Copyright Office, accessed March 8, 2021, https://www.copyright.gov/fair-use/more-info.html.

51 "Title IX and Sex Discrimination," US Department of Education Office for Civil Rights, revised June 2021, https://www2.ed.gov/about/offices/list/ocr/docs/tix_dis.html.

52 "Dear Colleague Letter," US Department of Education Office for Civil Rights, April 4, 2011, https://www2.ed.gov/about/offices/list/ocr/letters/colleague-201104.html.

53 Ken LaMance, "Clear and Convincing Evidence Standard," LegalMatch Law Library, May 3, 2018, https://www.legalmatch.com/law-library/article/clear-and-convincing-evidence-standard.html.

54 "Department of Education Issues New Interim Guidance on Campus Sexual Misconduct," US Department of Education, September 22, 2017, https://www.ed.gov/news/press-releases/department-education-issues-new-interim-guidance-campus-sexual-misconduct.

55 85 FR 30026, "Nondiscrimination on the Basis of Sex in Education Programs or Activities Receiving Federal Financial Assistance," US Department of Education, May 19, 2020, https://www.federalregister.gov/documents/2020/05/19/2020-10512/nondiscrimination-on-the-basis-of-sex-in-education-programs-or-activities-receiving-federal.

56 "Stony Brook University Code of Student Responsibility Sexual Misconduct Policy and Procedure," Stony Brook University, August 14, 2020, https://www.stonybrook.edu/commcms/oea-sexual-misconduct/_documents/SBU%20CoSR%20Sexual%20Misconduct%20Policy%20and%20Procedure.pdf.

57 "Students with Disabilities," National Center for Education Statistics, accessed March 21, 2021, https://nces.ed.gov/programs/coe/indicator_cgg.asp.

58 "Assistance For Education of All Children with Disabilities," 20 USC Chapter 33, Subchapter II, §1411, https://uscode.house.gov/view.xhtml?path=/prelim@title20/chapter33/subchapter2&edition=prelim.

59 Pam Wright and Pete Wright, Wrightslaw: From Emotions to Advocacy: The Special Education Survival Guide, 2nd edition (Hartfield, VA: Harbor House Law Press, 2006).

60 Marsha Weissan and Emily NaPier, Education Suspended: The Use of High School Disciplinary Records in College Admissions, Center for Community Alternatives, May 2015, http://www.communityalternatives.org/pdf/publications/EducationSuspended.pdf.

61 Weissan and NaPier, *Education Suspended.*

62 Weissan and NaPier, *Education Suspended.*

63 "Common App," Common App, accessed June 15, 2021, https://www.commonapp.org/,

64 "Conduct Records & Transcripts," Rutgers University Office of Student Conduct, accessed April 9, 2021, http://studentconduct.rutgers.edu/conduct-records-and-transcripts/.

65 *The Attorney General's Report on Criminal History Background Checks,* US Department of Justice, June 2006, http://www.bjs.gov/content/pub/pdf/ag_bgchecks_report.pdf.

66 "Criminal History Records: Additional Actions Could Enhance the Completeness of Records Used for Employment-Related Background Checks," US Government Accountability Office, March 16, 2015, https://www.gao.gov/products/gao-15-162.

CPSIA information can be obtained
at www.ICGtesting.com
Printed in the USA
BVHW091753021121
620556BV00015B/267

9 780578 985756